Character Education

A Guide for School Administrators

Edward F. DeRoche
Mary M. Williams

The Scarecrow Press, Inc.
A Scarecrow Education Book
Lanham, Maryland, and London
2001

SCARECROW PRESS, INC.
A Scarecrow Education Book

Published in the United States of America
by Scarecrow Press, Inc.
4720 Boston Way, Lanham, Maryland 20706
www.scarecroweducation.com

4 Pleydell Gardens, Folkestone
Kent CT20 2DN, England

Copyright © 2001 by Edward F. DeRoche and Mary M. Williams

All rights reserved. No part of this publication may be reproduced, stored in a retrieval system, or transmitted in any form or by any means, electronic, mechanical, photocopying, recording, or otherwise, without the prior permission of the publisher.

British Library Cataloguing in Publication Information Available

Library of Congress Cataloging-in-Publication Data

DeRoche, Edward F.
  Character education : a guide for school administrators / Edward F. DeRoche and Mary M. Williams.
    p. cm.
  Includes bibliographical references.
  ISBN 0-8108-3965-2 (alk. paper) — ISBN 0-8108-3960-1 (alk. paper)
  1. Moral education—United States—Handbooks, manuals, etc. I. Williams, Mary M. II. Title.

LC311.D46 2001
370.11'4'0973—dc21   00-051610

∞™ The paper used in this publication meets the minimum requirements of American National Standard for Information Sciences—Permanence of Paper for Printed Library Materials, ANSI/NISO Z39.48-1992.
Manufactured in the United States of America.

Contents

Acknowledgments *v*
Preface *vii*

1. The Comprehensive Framework — 1
2. Planning — 13
3. Leadership — 31
4. School Climate — 49
5. Teaching — 63
6. Training — 91
7. Programs — 111
8. Partnerships — 133
9. Evaluation — 149

Character Education Organizations *167*
Bibliography *173*
About the Authors *179*

Acknowledgments

For six years, Ed served on the California Commission on Teacher Credentialing. He dedicates this book to the CCTC administrators, staff, and commissioners particularly: Venna Dautenive, for her style, Torrie Norton for her administrative abilities, Scott Harvey for his analytical skills, Gary Reed for his political acumen, and Ned Sutro for his wit and wisdom.

Mary dedicates this book to her mother, Olga Williams, for her modeling of the ideal administrator described within. Her work in character education was developed by all the national and regional conferences and academies that have allowed her to test out ideas. She thanks her family for their support and patience with the process. She gives special thanks to all the administrators, teachers, parents, and school board members who have, over the years, analyzed and critiqued her ideas and practices.

The authors thank the following people for their permission to reprint original and/or copyrighted material: Marvin W. Berkowitz, Sanford N. McDonnell, Professor of Character Education; Esther F. Schaeffer, Executive Director, Character Education Partnership; Henry Huffman, Director of the Character Education Institute at California University of Pennsylvania; Elizabeth Sutherland, teacher at Lucy V. Barnsley Elementary School (Rockville, Maryland); and John Forenti, Character Counts! Coordinator, Tulare County Office of Education.

Much praise goes to our competent and talented editor, Patricia Waldygo, and our graduate fellow at the University of San Diego, Jenny Ferrone. We thank both of you.

Edward DeRoche
Mary Williams

Preface

Leadership is the conjunction of good ideas and good character. One without the other is unsustainable.

—Jim Leach, Congressman, Iowa

OUR JOURNEY

We began our character education journey long before arriving to teach and administer at the university level. For both of us, it began in our relationships with our families and friends, and in our experiences at schools and in neighborhoods. Early in our careers as teachers and administrators, we believed we were educators concerned with the moral development of the students we met and worked with over the years. Each of us, in our own way, addressed the character development of our students. As part of our professorial lives, we studied and wrote on this important topic. It all came together when we met at the University of San Diego and engaged in conversations about character education, moral development, values, and virtues. Our readings and experiences conducting staff-development workshops, graduate seminars, and speeches at conferences expanded the content of our conversations to the point where we decided that we should do something together, so we decided to write a book proposal.

In early 1998, Corwin Press published our book *Educating Hearts and Minds: A Comprehensive Character Education Framework*.[1] Shortly before the book was published, Mary was asked to chair the Association of Teacher Educators' Commission on Character Education and Ed became a member of the Commission. ATE published a journal on the theme of character education with Mary as an editor[2] and followed up later that year with the Report of the Commission on Character Education.[3] Ed, who has had a long-standing interest in the use of daily newspapers in the classroom, published a workbook titled *Character Matters: Strategies for Teachers, Activities for Parents*.[4] The journey continued with opportunities for both of us to write, consult, make presentations, and conduct workshops for P–12 educators on topics related to character education.

During this time, we "mapped" out an idea for an International Center for Character Education (ICCE) at the University of San Diego. Mal Rafferty, the director of the Division of Continuing Education, shared our vision that the center's major activities should be an outreach to the education community. Under his direction, teacher workshops were created throughout California so that we could share the character education message. We believed that teachers are character educators whether they want to be or not. We also believed that it is best for teachers to receive training to be character educators.

So, we went "on the road." Over a five-month period, we conducted, together or individually, workshops that introduced teachers and others to the idea that it is important to attend to the character development of children and youth in schools. We interacted with hundreds of teachers. We made presentations at state and national conferences. Then, in June 1999, ICCE had its first international conference and academy on character education with more than 300 educators participating. This successful conference/academy on character education was repeated in June 2000.

These experiences have been informative, rewarding, and sometimes discouraging. We are now certain that teachers in training, classroom teachers, administrators, and school counselors benefit from background information and knowledge of the underlying principles and understanding of their role as character educators. We also learned from veteran teachers and others that they perceived three problems: parents, principals, and an overloaded curriculum. Many teachers expressed concern about support from their principals. Some said that they were hesitant about implementing a program without knowing how parents would respond. Some administrators said that their focus had to be on raising the achievement levels of students—test scores are what counts in their community and with the media. They did not know, and many did not believe, that there is a relationship between educating for good character and academic achievement.

On the other hand, some teachers and administrators expressed their strong belief that the character education program in their schools and classrooms was contributing to better behavior and higher student achievement. All agreed that if the school principal did not support character education, then it would not take hold. Time and again, our conversations led back to the school principal. For some principals the question was, "How do I start it in my school?" For others, it was, "How do I maintain the momentum of this new program?" For a few, the question was, "How do we evaluate the program and student learning and report the results to the school board and the public?"

As is our style, we had many personal conversations about administrative leadership for character education. We read. We talked with teachers and administrators. We concluded that a book for school administrators was necessary. As luck would have it, just as we were starting to record some of our questions and ideas, Dr. Joseph Eckenrode, vice president of Technomic Publishing, contacted us and asked if we were interested in submitting a proposal for a book on the topic.

Yes, we were interested and would submit a proposal. So, we squeezed time into our already-busy schedules to do it. The proposal was accepted and we began our journey to write the manuscript.

THIS BOOK

We wanted a book that was different from the usual texts on school administration. We wanted a book that had a different format, one that would be practical, useful, and easy to read. We wanted this book to build on the comprehensive character education framework that we developed earlier and that needed refining. We also wanted a book worth reading, a book that would help administrators "do" character education and show school principals how to implement the framework.

To prepare to write this book, we decided to spend some time going through business books in local bookstores. We liked the way many of these books provided advice and counsel in a nontextbook format. We scanned more than thirty how-to books in the business field. We analyzed the content and studied the format. We selected several books that not only shaped some of the content included in this book, but also gave us ideas for unique, interesting, and readable formats. We found that the authors of these books use stories, outlines, charts, bullets, checklists, graphics, and other schema to help the reader. We did the same. As you will note, we use a tour as our metaphor. We got the idea from Lehmann's book *Driver's Ed for Today's Managers.*[5] We also use alliteration and other memory devices to help you, the busy school administrator, remember the essential points, implement our suggestions, try our activities, and lead your constituents to a successful and comprehensive character education program.

YOUR MAP, OUR BOOK

We quote and paraphrase Lehmann's suggestions[6] that today's leaders, particularly in schools, must:

1. Drive for results; caring, civil, and challenging schools, both academically and behaviorally, through effective leadership and coaching.
2. Share their knowledge and leadership with others in the school and the school's community.
3. Help teachers, students, parents, and others do their best work by providing opportunities and resources.
4. Look to the future—shape it, help others do the same, and answer the question "What can adults do to make a school the best it can be for the students who attend it?"

As we laid out the map for this book, we had two primary objectives:

Objective One: To give you the essential information you need to guide your school on its journey to comprehensive, effective, and successful character education initiatives.

Objective Two: To highlight your importance as a leader for the school's character education initiatives.

OUR BOOK, YOUR JOURNEY

"Experience and common sense suggest that if education is to do the things the public says it should do, it must be accomplished at the building level. Educational change will be most effective when it resides with the principal, teachers, students, and parents in the individual school."[7] Replace the words "educational change" with "character education" and the importance of what happens at a school site is underscored. As one famous politician put it: "All politics is local." So, too, are school-reform efforts, one of which is character education. We emphasize the school site because everyone knows and has experienced the diversity among schools sites (economically, socially, and culturally) within the same school district. The road to improving the character of students leads to the school site, where parents'/guardians' interests and involvement are the greatest.

You should note that we have replaced the chapter designation with "tour stop" to stay with our travel metaphor. We recommend that you scan the entire book first, so that before you start reading it sequentially, you will have an overall picture of the journey.

Your character education journey will begin at Tour Stop 1 with a review of a "new" comprehensive framework that we created as a result of studying successful character education programs.

We arrange the second tour stop to be a way for you to plan and find out from your constituents what they want the school-community core values to be. These core values will underpin the school's character education initiatives. In other words, at Tour Stop 2, we want you to be sure that everyone is on the same tour bus, going in the same direction. You want all your stakeholders to come to a consensus about the values and their definitions, and to identify their expectations for this character education trip.

At Tour Stop 3, we take the main road for this journey and share some important ideas about your responsibilities, your leadership, your vision, and the program's mission, goals, and expectations. This information will help you in your role as the character education tour guide.

Tour Stop 4 addresses school climate. If you have been on a tour, you know that the value of the tour is determined by the quality of the buses, the hotels, the sites visited, the meals, and the atmosphere created by the tour guide. We will advise you on how to create a school climate that supports the school's character education efforts.

Tour Stop 5 is the place where we reflect upon the all-important teaching of the core values. We talk about teaching strategies and instructional methods that deliver the essence of the school's character education program in ways that foster the character development of students.

At Tour Stop 6, we present you with the essential task of training school personnel about the need for and the challenges and preparation required to create and deliver a quality, effective character education program.

The central elements of a character education program will be reviewed at Tour Stop 7. At this stop we describe school-wide activities, curricular and co-curricular matters, and selected character education programs.

As your character education trip continues, you will visit Tour Stop 8, which is about forming relationships that will support the program. This is the "partnerships" stop. We have some advice and counsel about forming strong, effective partners for your school's character education efforts.

Like any tour, one looks back and reflects on its value. What was memorable? What were the highlights? What could have been better? What went wrong? At Tour Stop 9, the last stop on our character education tour, we offer guidelines and examples for evaluating your school's character education initiatives. This stop will end our character education tour with you. But for you and others at your school and in your community, it will be the beginning of a new and rewarding journey on the road to helping students become people of good character.

Each tour stop concludes with resources for you to use and to share with others. They are resources for those who will be active participants in your school's character education journey.

On Tour: We visit schools and people who have made changes that have contributed to the climate of their school and the character of their students. It should be noted here that in order to meet the needs of storytelling, we have modified and embellished the references used without altering the facts.

Tour Readings: At each stop we identify books and articles we think are particularly useful and helpful.

Tour Web Sites: These sites will be as valuable a resource for you as they have been to us.

YOUR LEADERSHIP—DRIVING THE BUS

Leadership is the central theme that runs through the discussions at each of the tour stops in this book. You are the school's character education tour guide. Your role is to lead as well as facilitate, plan, organize, manage, and assess the character education initiatives at your school.

We cannot emphasize enough the importance of school principals as leaders for character education initiatives. For this reason, we want to tell you something about your role and responsibilities as leader of the school's character education efforts.

What are the expectations for a principal who wants to "lead" his or her school's character education initiatives? Here are the criteria for getting your character education leadership license.

1. Lay the groundwork for creating and implementing the school's character education initiatives.

2. Get stakeholders involved in all aspects of the program.
3. Ensure that stakeholders reach consensus on the values and agree to their definitions.
4. Share leadership responsibilities and empower the stakeholders.
5. Be the visionary and missionary for the school's character education program.
6. Be a coach, communicator, and collaborator.
7. Lead by example—model the values and encourage stakeholders to follow your lead.
8. Be a risk-taker and problem solver and help stakeholders do the same.
9. Lead by being a monitor, auditor, and reporter.

Heifetz,[8] in his book on leadership, uses the dance metaphor. He says that those engaged in the dance may not see the patterns made by the dancers. The music, the motions, one's partner, spacing, and the need to attend to what one is doing may capture their attention. "To discern the large patterns on the dance floor—to see who is dancing with whom, in what groups, in what location, and who is sitting out which kind of dance—we have to stop moving and get to the balcony."

Somebody (we'll suggest a character education council and a character education evaluation team) has to get to the "balcony" and take pictures. Somebody will have to take snapshots along the character education trip. These will be useful for recording patterns, moods, perceptions, highlights, and low points. But the real value comes when you and others decide just how well these snapshots capture the real picture and accurately reflect the sights and sounds of places visited. Then you and others can arrange the snapshots in an album that will give the public and stakeholders a sense of whether the character education trip was worthwhile, what changes have to be made, and how these changes should be implemented for the next trip.

Gordon Vessels, a school psychologist and character education researcher in the Atlanta public schools, gives us the bottom line, one about which we wholeheartedly agree: "I concluded very early in the process that success depends upon character education becoming the highest priority for the school principal. In schools where principals did not make character education their highest priority. . . less positive change was observed."[9]

Fasten your seatbelt and have a good trip!

REFERENCES

1. E. F. DeRoche and M. M. Williams, *Educating Hearts and Minds: A Comprehensive Character Education Framework* (Thousand Oaks, CA: Corwin Press, 1998).

2. M. M. Williams and E. Schaps, eds., "Character Education," in *Action in Teacher Education* (Alexandria, VA: Association of Teacher Education, 1999a).

3. M. M. Williams and E. Schaps, eds., *Character Education: The Foundation for Teacher Education*. The Report of the ATE National Commission on Character Education (Washington, DC: Character Education Partnership, 1999b).

4. E. F. DeRoche, *Character Matters: Strategies for Teachers, Activities for Parents* (San Francisco, CA: USETHENEWS Foundation, 2000).

5. H. Lehmann, *Driver's Ed for Today's Managers* (Auburn, WA: Organizational Performance & Planning Institute, 1998).

6. H. Lehmann, *Driver's Ed for Today's Managers* (Auburn, WA: Organizational Performance & Planning Institute, 1998), 7.

7. E. F. DeRoche, *An Administrator's Guide for Evaluating Programs and Personnel* (Boston, MA: Allyn & Bacon, 1981), 3–4.

8. R. Heifetz, *Leadership without Easy Answers* (Cambridge, MA: Harvard University Press, 1994), 253.

9. G. Vessels, *Character Education and Community Development* (Westport, CT: Praeger, 1998), 162.

• *Tour Stop 1* •

The Comprehensive Framework

> *Check the records. All great failures in life are character failures, and all complete successes are character based. The [need] for character education is irrefutable.*
>
> —Zig Ziglar, in B. D. Brooks, *The Case for Character Education* (1997)

The question is: How can you best prepare for the character education journey? Our answer is in this chapter. While the centerpiece of this tour stop is a character education framework, that framework will take on greater meaning when you have the "big picture" of what character education is about. The framework is supported by recommendations from the experts. The framework is an organizational pattern that we recommend you consider for your school.

CHARACTER EDUCATION MANIFESTO

The "Character Education Manifesto" is an excellent guiding rationale that can be very helpful in getting stakeholders to understand the significance of character education. We suggest that you share it with others as you are forming your school's character education committees. There are some important events that you may find helpful, when giving background information to a school board or group of educators, that led up to the Character Education Manifesto. In chronological order they are as follows:

- ☑ The Association for Supervision and Curriculum Development, Princeton Project 55, and the Johnson Foundation co-sponsored a conference at Wingspread in Racine, Wisconsin in March 1992, to give priority to character education.
- ☑ The Josephson Institute of Ethics sponsored a meeting in Aspen, Colorado in July 1992. Thirty national leaders developed a common set of values designed to transcend cultural, political, economic, and religious lines. The group agreed to promote the common set of values through greater involvement with children and youth.

Effective character education is based on core ethical values which form the foundation of a democratic society.

(Aspen Declaration, 1992)[1]

- ☑ 1993: The Character Education Partnership was formed. This national, nonprofit, nonpartisan coalition's main purpose is dedicated to developing good character and civic virtue in young people.
- ☑ 1993: The Josephson Institute of Ethics established the Character Counts! Coalition. The coalition gathers support from business, political, educational, and religious leaders to foster what they call the "Six Pillars of Character"—trustworthiness, responsibility, caring, respect for others, fairness, and citizenship.
- ☑ 1994, 1995, 1996, and 1997: The Communitarian Network hosted White House–sponsored conferences on "Character-Building for a Civil and Democratic Society."
- ☑ 1995: The U.S. Department of Education supported character education planning grants in four states—California, Iowa, New Mexico, and Utah. By the year 2000, twenty-four more grants were awarded to state departments of education.
- ☑ 1996: Phi Delta Kappa International established the League of Values-Driven Schools. The league was created to foster the development of positive beliefs among students, educators, and parents. The league has invited high schools to become participants in promoting the values of learning, honesty, cooperation, service to others, freedom, responsibility, and civility.

☑ 1996: Several of the major players in the character education movement signed the Character Education Manifesto, suggesting "guiding principles" that ought to be central to education reform. In summary, these principles are that:

- Education is a moral enterprise requiring a continuous and conscious effort to guide students to know and pursue what is good and what is worthwhile.
- Parents are the primary moral educators, and schools should build partnerships with the home to foster students' personal and civic virtues, such as integrity, courage, responsibility, diligence, service, and respect for the dignity of all persons.
- Character education is about developing virtues; it is not about acquiring the right views.
- The school principal, teachers, and all other school personnel must be educated about, embody, and reflect upon the moral authority invested in them by parents and the community.
- Character education is an integral part of school life, in which the school becomes a community of virtue fostering modeling, teaching, expecting, celebrating, and practicing responsibility, hard work, honesty, and kindness.
- Teachers and students draw from the moral wisdom that exists in our great stories, works of art, literature, history, and biography.
- The sum of young people's school experiences provides much of the raw material that forges their own characters.[2]

This manifesto, in our opinion, provides you with a holistic view of the importance of character education in schools. We think it is worth a second reading. We suggest that you reread it and share it with others from time to time as you go about developing your school's character education program.

Certain basic principles are important to you and to the stakeholders for guiding the character education initiatives at your school and establishing board policy.

ELEVEN PRINCIPLES

Three leaders in the character education movement, Tom Lickona, Eric Schaps, and Catherine Lewis, developed eleven principles that serve as criteria for effective character education efforts. We summarize them here for your review. The full statements for each of the eleven principles may be obtained from the Character Education Partnership or by viewing their Web site. The important point here is that these eleven principles, like the manifesto, give you the overview you need as the school's principal and leader to get your school ready for its character education work.

1. Character education promotes core ethical values as a basis of good character.
2. "Character" must be comprehensively defined to include thinking, feeling, and behavior.
3. Effective character education requires an intentional, proactive, and comprehensive approach that promotes the core values in all phases of school life.
4. The school must be a caring community.
5. To develop character, students need opportunities for moral action.
6. Effective character education includes a meaningful and challenging academic curriculum that respects all learners and helps them succeed.
7. Character education should strive to develop students' intrinsic motivation.
8. The school staff must become a learning and moral community in which all share responsibility for character education and attempt to adhere to the same core values that guide the education of students.
9. Character education requires moral leadership from both students and staff.
10. The school must recruit parents and community members as full partners in the character-building effort.
11. Evaluation of character education should assess the character of the school, the school staff's functioning as character educators, and the extent to which students manifest good character.[3]

The manifesto and eleven principles serve as a useful preamble to the components of the framework that will be discussed next.

We must provide a comprehensive and intelligent blueprint for putting our schools back on track.

(William Kilpatrick, 1993)[4]

A COMPREHENSIVE FRAMEWORK

When we began our study and examination of the character education literature and various programs in the mid-'90s, we noted an absence of a comprehensive framework that might be a useful template for school personnel and community leaders. The framework we developed in 1998 highlighted the following components: vision, standards, expectations, criteria, leadership, resources, training, partnerships, and assessment. Further study and conversations with practitioners and character education specialists motivated us to modify our original framework for the second edition of *Educating Hearts and Minds*.[5]

As we worked on this book, which is addressed specifically to school administrators, we decided to modify the framework once again, and compare it to that proposed by Ryan and Bohlin.[6] Figure 1.1 shows both frameworks.

Ryan and Bohlin's Framework	DeRoche and Williams' Framework
o Mission	o Planning
o Core virtues	o Leadership
o Partnerships	o School Climate
o Teamwork	o Teaching
o Implementation	o Training
o Meetings and assessment	o Programs
o Staff development	o Partnerships
o Student involvement	o Evaluation
o Integrating activities	
o Evaluation	

Figure 1.1

Each of the components in our framework is a "tour stop" in this book. Resources and standards are crucial and underscore all of the components of the framework. Each tour stop ends with a list of recommended references so that at different parts of this journey you will have information you can refer to that expands and enriches our discussion of that particular component.

Thus, the framework that we are recommending looks like this.

It became apparent to us that effective character education programs have common components. We found these components of the framework in comprehensive character education initiatives. Each component performs a unique process or function, yet contains common interlocking content and forms significant relationships. We did not find successful

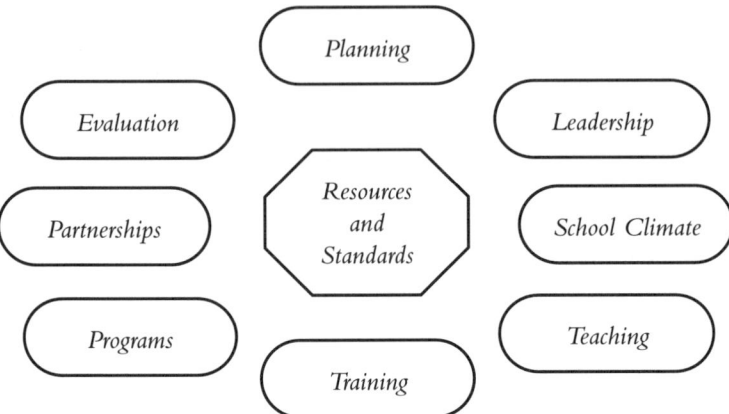

Figure 1.2 The Comprehensive Character Education Framework

character education programs where only a few of the components were present; thus, we concluded that all of them were essential.

As you look over the components for an effective character education framework, you will note that they fit into what you already know about effective schooling, leadership, and strategic planning. What makes this framework unique is that once you read the content for each component, you will see that it captures the main thrust of the manifesto, as well as the eleven principles, and helps to establish broad policies. We believe that a unique feature of the framework is its flexibility. We expect that you and your colleagues will make decisions about adapting or adjusting each of the components based on your school's needs, priorities, and access to resources. We believe that the connections between all of the components, properly applied, will help make for an effective and comprehensive character education program in your school.

 *Character education has moved to a point where the majority of society is beginning to see the need for a community approach rather than an approach that leaves individual families and institutions working in isolation.*

(Brooks, 1995)

ORGANIZATION

Our discussions with school administrators about how best to organize personnel for the school's character education efforts suggest that the following pattern may be useful. Depending on the size of your school, we recommend three committees. One might be called the Character Education Council (CEC); the second, the Character Education Evaluation Team (CEET); and the third, the Character Education Partnership Team (CEPT).

Both CEET and CEPT report to the CEC, which has the overall responsibility for the school's character education efforts. We believe that the amount of work required to create and maintain partnerships and to assess the program requires additional personnel. In schools that do not have many school personnel, the CEC would have to take on the responsibilities of forming partnerships and doing program evaluation. These three committees will be referred to regularly as we progress through this journey.

The membership on each committee must be broad-based; that is, representatives from as many groups as possible should be on each committee. Certainly, the CEC should have teachers, staff, administrators, parents, and community members assuming the overall responsibilities for the school and the community's character education program.

Our point is this—as the school principal, you cannot lead and administer the character education program without representation from the stakeholders. They need to be involved. They need to take leadership roles. They also need to help you carve out policies and practices that will help make the program meet its expectations and goals. You will have to decide which organizational pattern is best for your school and which works for you. We are suggesting one pattern. Many more are possible, as you will note when you read the recommended books and articles.

TOUR TIPS

We end this tour stop about readiness and organization by sharing with you a paraphrase of "18 Secret Tips for Effective Character Education," offered by Marvin W. Berkowitz, who is the Sanford N. McDonnell Professor of Character Education at the University of Missouri at St. Louis.

A. To educate for goodness means to educate for a lot of different things, which means using a variety of methods.
B. Character develops slowly, often in stages, so design support efforts and expectations accordingly.
C. Character education combines how you do it with what you do!
D. Students need support, guidance, and tutelage to develop character.
E. Relationships are the most powerful element in character education.

F. Discovery learning, *constructivism,* and *problem-based learning* are the recommended methods in character development (italics ours).
G. When all voices are heard and valued, empowerment, commitment, and ownership result.
H. To promote character development, engage students in conversations about character and moral issues.
I. High, attainable, and supported expectations promote character development.
J. Character education is not an add-on, it is the transformation of the culture of the school.
K. Teaching for character is similar to being a good parent.
L. Since character development happens slowly and in stages, think long term in your planning and goals.
M. The principal's support is essential for successful character education.
N. Leadership of the character education program must be shared; stakeholders must be empowered.
O. One must understand "the unit of the system" most appropriate for program implementation:

- In elementary schools it's the classroom;
- In middle schools it's the team; and
- At the high school level it's the whole school community, not departments.

P. Students think about and see the world differently than adults. Effective character education captures their visions.
Q. It really does help to have "the village help to raise the child."

TOUR THOUGHTS

Our intent at this first tour stop was to "educate" you about the many facets of character education. We turned off at the "vista point" so you could look across the character education "valley" and see the view—the whole picture. The manifesto gives you the vision and the purposes for character education. The eleven principles set the boundaries for the framework. Each of the components seen on the horizon are the tour stops you take as you read this book. Once you get the people on the tour bus, get your committees arranged and think about our "travel tips." The first stop "on tour" gives you a "snapshot" of a comprehensive Board of Education policy about character education. Now, while we are giving you the overview and getting you "up-to-speed" on the topic, before you start this character education trip, we remind you that others are on the tour bus with you. They, too, need to be prepared for this tour. Therefore, we strongly suggest that you share the information at this tour stop with those stakeholders in your school who will be on this tour with you. The next stop is the planning phase, which will ensure that your trip is successful.

On our first tour stop in this book, we drive to the Montgomery County Public School (Maryland) office.[7] We stop to pick up a copy of the Board of Education's comprehensive policy on character education because we think is it one that all "tourists" should have as they begin their character education journey. This statement can guide you in developing your school's mission statement and program goals. Approved on February 10, 1998, the policy states:

> The Board of Education believes that every child's character is molded by influences starting with the child's family and including all the institutions that affect the child's life. It is a major purpose of public education to teach, model, and encourage in every possible way the development of good character in every child.
>
> A. Purpose:
>   1. To reaffirm the Board of Education's commitment to the ideals of good character and citizenship through character education, which shall include, but not be limited to, the following: caring and consideration for others, citizenship, fairness, hard work, honesty, respect, responsibility, trustworthiness, and integrity.
>   2. To ensure that character education programs address the unique needs of the individual school communities through the collaboration of staff, students, parents, and the greater school community.
>   3. To continue to foster a safe, supportive, and academically challenging environment for all students by providing skills for personal interaction based on living in and contributing to a democratic society.

B. Issue:

The Montgomery County Public Schools value the right of every child to receive a quality education. The Board of Education recognizes that a quality education includes a fundamental expectation that schools provide an environment that encourages the development of a strong moral anchor in truth, responsibility, and justice. American public education has historically viewed character development as a foundation of the major mission of successful teaching and learning. The social environments of homes, schools, and communities form values and character. Clear expectations and pride in complying with the norms of the community help shape behavior. Families, schools, and communities have a profound influence on character, ethics, and values in both direct and indirect ways, and school communities have a responsibility to teach, demonstrate, and promote ethical behavior. All stakeholders in the education process must work in partnership to ensure the successful development of the citizens of future generations.

C. Position:
1. Character education shall include, but not be limited to, the following: caring and consideration of others, citizenship, fairness, hard work, honesty, respect, responsibility, trustworthiness, and integrity.
2. The Board of Education expects staff, students, families, and the greater community to engage in a deliberate process to determine the additional specific character education components that reflect their unique school/cluster community.
3. School communities shall be maintained in which positive behavior is practiced, demonstrated, modeled, and reinforced within an environment of mutual respect and dignity.
4. The Montgomery County Public Schools *Program of Studies* shall provide opportunities for the integration of character education throughout the curricula.

D. Desired Outcomes:
1. Character education is a foundation of the schools' major mission of successful teaching and learning.
2. Students are prepared to live and contribute as citizens in a democratic society.
3. Families, schools, and communities work in partnership to model and develop qualities of good character and ethical decision-making abilities.

E. Implementation Strategies:
1. Schools will continue to provide opportunities for students to demonstrate and practice good character.
2. Every school shall have a program to support efforts to build good character.
3. The process of integrating character education in school-wide programs will include the involvement of students, staff, families, and the greater school community.
4. Student expectations are articulated in Policy JFA: *Student Rights and Responsibilities.* (Note that number 4 is in italics.)
5. Staff members are expected to model good character and citizenship and ethical decision-making.
6. The superintendent shall recommend any changes to the *Program of Studies* that may be necessary to include character education objectives in the instructional program.
7. Regulations to implement this policy will be developed as necessary.

E. L. Boyer, *The Basic School: A Community for Learning* (Princeton, NJ: The Carnegie Foundation for the Advancement of Teaching, 1995).

B. D. Brooks, *The Case for Character Education* (Northridge, CA: Studio 4 Productions, 1997).

E. F. DeRoche and M. M. Williams, *Educating Hearts and Minds: A Comprehensive Character Education Framework,* 2d ed. (Thousand Oaks, CA: Corwin Press, 2001).

K. Ryan and K. Bohlin, *Building Character in Schools* (San Francisco, CA: Jossey-Bass, 1999).

P. F. Vincent, *Developing Character in Students* (Chapel Hill, NC: View Publications, 1996).

Character Education Partnership, *http://www.character.org.*
International Center for Character Education, *http://teachvalues.org.*

REFERENCES

1. *Aspen Declaration* (unpublished document, 1992).
2. *Character Education Manifesto* (Center for the Advancement of Ethics and Character, http://education.bu.edu/charactered, 1998), 3.
3. E. Schaps, T. Lickona, and C. Lewis, *Eleven Principles of Effective Character Education* (Alexandria, VA: Character Education Partnership, 1996).
4. W. Kilpatrick, "cover quote." In E. Wynne and K. Ryan, *Reclaiming Our Schools: A Handbook on Teaching Character, Academics, and Discipline* (New York, NY: Macmillan Publishing Co., 1993).
5. E. F. DeRoche and M. M. Williams, *Educating Hearts and Minds: A Comprehensive Character Education Framework,* 2d ed. (Thousand Oaks, CA: Corwin Press, 2001).
6. K. Ryan and K. Bohlin, *Building Character in Schools* (San Francisco, CA: Jossey-Bass, 1999).
7. Montgomery Public Schools, Board Minutes (Montgomery Public Schools, February 10, 1998).

• *Tour Stop 2* •

Planning

> *The first concern most people have is . . . whose values system will be taught? Who is to say what is right and what is wrong? Who are you to tell me or my child what is right or wrong?*
>
> —L. Wiley, *Comprehensive Character Building Classroom: A Handbook for Teachers*, 1998

Tours and journeys begin with much anticipation and varied expectations. Your character education journey will be similar in many respects. We will assume that there is a need for you, and those at your school, to take this tour to create a new character education program or improve the one you have. As you well know, all "packaged" tours are carefully crafted and well planned. So, here is our plan for you at this tour stop. We will begin by answering some frequently asked questions. The first set of questions consists of pre-planning ones. The next six are questions most frequently asked of us. These will be followed by a discussion about expectations and outcomes. Then we will provide a strategy that will help you and your stakeholders decide which values will be the core values underpinning the school's character education efforts. We give you some examples of how others define these values so you do not have to "reinvent the wheel." Then, we end this tour stop with a program standards checklist.

PRE-PLANNING

It is important to take stock of what you are already doing and then think about the kinds of resources that you are going to need in your school.

Prepare yourself in advance by answering the following questions:

Four Questions to Answer before Planning a Character Education Program

1. What is the climate of your school like?
2. Which values does your school explicitly promote, and how are these values taught?
3. What are the expectations of parents regarding citizenship, behavior, and achievement?
4. What are your school's measures of success?

Your responses to these questions can help shape the list of expectations for your current program or for planning a new character education program. If your school builds upon what you already do well, you are more likely to implement a program to which stakeholders will feel committed. Now is the time to step back and take a good look at what you are already doing before beginning a new journey.

1. What is the climate of your school?

    Tour Stop 4 discusses school climate in some detail. As a means of introducing the component of "climate," we remind you that it is made up of the physical and human elements of an organization. How well the human interactions play out within the school environment determines whether your climate is a positive or negative one. Be honest! What impression do you get when you walk through the front door of the school? In fact, step back, and notice what someone else might see as he or she walks through the school entrance. Do you have a clear picture in mind? Is the physical environment pleasant? Is the lighting good? What does the physical plant tell you about your school?

    Next, look with fresh eyes at interactions and relationships. Following are some questions to ask yourself:

    - Is the atmosphere a pleasant one in which to work?
    - Are teachers' and administrators' working relationships positive?
    - Are teachers working collaboratively?
    - Are students well behaved and hardworking?
    - How would you describe the relationships between teachers and students?
    - Are parents welcome in the school?

- Do you see parents or other community members around the school on a typical day, or is their presence rare?

At Tour Stop 4, we suggest ways you can improve and assess your school's climate. The next step in pre-planning is to list the values that are already being promoted in your school.

2. Which values does your school explicitly promote, and how are they taught?

Values are taught intentionally and unintentionally, in classrooms and in hallways. So, you need to look at the climate (hidden curriculum) and the actual lessons that permeate the whole school and individual classrooms. If your school climate is positive, it is likely that the values learned by the students are positive personal and prosocial/civic ones. If your school climate is neutral or negative, it is likely that students are getting mixed messages about important values, behaviors, and expectations.

Reflect on the answers to these questions:

- What specific curricular and co-curricular activities do your students participate in that teach them positive personal values and prosocial behaviors?
- What programs are you implementing that contribute to students' character development?
- What special activities does your school promote that contribute to student leadership opportunities?
- What programs are offered that require students to provide service to others?
- Which clubs and after-school programs are successful?

Take a few minutes, right now, and list the values that you think students learn in your school, and make a note about how they learn them. This information can help when you begin planning.

3. What are the current expectations of parents?

An overwhelming preponderance of evidence gathered in Gallup polls since 1983[1] indicates that parents believe that public schools should be teaching values, such as respect, fairness, responsibility, and honesty. In our experience, there is agreement by educators, parents, and community members about a core of values to teach children in schools. The only time we have heard of resistance from parents toward character education efforts, or the teaching of values in schools, is when parents have not been included in the consensus-building activities. They resist what they do not know. It is absolutely essential that parents be included in planning and discussions and have a sense that their voices and opinions matter. So, what do the parents think about student behavior and achievement at your school? How do you think parents will feel about character education? Do parents need to be prepared (educated) about character education? At Tour Stop 8, you will find examples of how parents are included as essential partners in a school's character education initiatives.

 "Let us push the case further by posing three questions: If not civility, what? If not schools, where? If not now, when?"

(Kauffman and Burbach, 1997)[2]

4. What are your school's measures of success?

The sample questions that follow can serve as a guide to help you assess the success of character education efforts.

- What is the rate of student misbehavior in school?
- What is the level of student achievement on standardized tests?
- What is the absentee rate for students?
- What are the number of bullying and fighting incidents?
- What is the rate of parental support?

The most important question is: What are your school's current measures of success? Answers to all these questions will help you and your stakeholders take a snapshot of what is happening at your school before you begin a character education program. We strongly recommend that you look at the students' behaviors, in addition to looking at test scores. Look closely at all student learning outcomes. The purpose of posing assessment questions early is that you can take more snapshots at the end of each year, compare the results, and communicate the gains/losses to parents and board members. Nothing is more convincing to stakeholders than before/after reporting. Taking snapshots, that is, measuring the success of your school's character education efforts, is developed more fully at Tour Stop 9.

Planning 17

SIX FAQS

As your school's tour guide, you need to be prepared to answer questions that will arise about character education. Here are six frequently asked questions (FAQs) that have been asked of us during workshops, seminars, and academies.

Character Education
Six FAQs by Workshop Participants:

1. What is character?
2. What is a value?
3. Which values are we talking about?
4. Why teach values in the public schools?
5. What is character education?
6. Does character education really work?

1. What is character?

There are many definitions of character and you should keep some of these handy for a quick response to your stakeholders.

Character is knowing the good, desiring the good, and doing the good. Or said another way—habits of the mind, habits of the heart, and habits of action. (Thomas Lickona)

Character is the sum of our intellectual and moral habits—our good habits or virtues, our bad habits or vices—the habits that make us the kind of person we are. (Kevin Ryan)

The true test of character is not how much we know how to do, but how we behave when we don't know what to do. (John Holt)

The measure of a person's real character is what s/he would do if s/he knew s/he would never be found out. (Thomas Macaulay)

Character is a function of one's sense of right and wrong, one's standard of what is good and just, and one's judgment of what constitutes good and bad human behavior. (Richard Sparks, Jr.)

Character is how you behave in response to the company you keep—seen and unseen. (Robert Coles)

We usually end this question by asking our audience members what they think Martin Luther King, Jr., meant when he said that our children should "live in a nation where they will not be judged by the color of their skin but by the content of their character."

2. What is a value?

A value is a preference, an ideal that guides our behavior, and something we try to live up to. Values lay the foundation for the acquisition of moral knowledge and inform us about ways in which to behave or not to behave. For each value, there is a vice (e.g., honesty: dishonesty). The individual nature of values may mislead people to think that anything goes. This conception is false and socially disastrous (Talbot and Tate, 1997).[3]

What is important is that children develop values and character traits that make it possible for people to live harmoniously and at peace. This is especially critical as the world continues to move toward instantaneous global communication and interaction.

(Brooks, 1997)[4]

3. Which values are we talking about?

To answer this question, we usually cite state laws or education codes that include values in their mandates. In addition, we also describe the requirements in federal government incentives for states in their funding of character education projects. One of our favorite responses is to cite the work of the Baltimore (Maryland) County Public Schools Task Force on Values and Ethical Behavior (1989). The Task Force's analysis of the two framing documents for the U.S. Constitution and the Declaration of Independence revealed twenty-four core values. The following values form the basis of their character education program: compassion, courtesy, critical inquiry, due process, equality of opportunity, freedom of thought and action, honesty, human worth and dignity, integrity, justice, knowledge, loyalty, objectivity, order, patriotism, rational consent, respect for other's rights, responsible citizenship, rule of law, self-respect, tolerance, and truth.

The values to be taught in your school should be the ones generated through consensus-building activities (see p. 23). We have found that mandated values imposed from the outside do not have the same buy-in by stakeholders that mutually agreed-upon values have, even if you end up with the same values.

4. Why teach values in the public schools?

Students need guidance from parents and other adults. They need opportunities to discuss why personal and civic values chosen by the school and community are important. They need to understand how behaviors relate to core values. Above all, they need to practice applying the values in and out of school.

Here is our "short list" of reasons for teaching values in your school:

- ☑ It benefits students, families, and the community.
- ☑ It enhances prosocial behaviors.
- ☑ It develops moral understanding in students.
- ☑ It helps students learn to make informed decisions.
- ☑ It helps prepare students to work in groups with others of different backgrounds and abilities.
- ☑ It creates benchmarks against which students can "test" their behaviors and evaluate the behaviors of others.
- ☑ It educates students that members of a democratic society are pledged to uphold a set of personal and civic values.

The importance of the social and ethical values that children experience in the classroom—the values that are modeled and lived there—cannot be overemphasized: children need to experience fairness, respect, responsibility, . . . and kindness in order to reciprocate such behavior.

(Dalton and Watson, 1997)[5]

5. What is character education?

Without a standard definition for character education, you may get lost on your journey. We prefer taking a panoramic view of character education. Here is a summary of our view presented in workshops and seminars:

> We believe that character education begins at home. We believe that parents are the primary character educators. We believe that children and youth learn values by observing and modeling the behavior of the adults around them. Sizer and Sizer (1999)[6] aptly capture this phrase in the title of their book *The Children Are Watching*. Children and youth learn values by listening to adults struggle with problems, thinking through dilemmas, and sharing ideas with their peers. Children and youth learn values by practicing them, taking action, and reflecting on how those actions affect others around them. This means that character education naturally extends from the home into the schools and the community.

Following are other definitions that may be useful in your planning:

> The National Commission on Character Education[7] offers a broad definition of character education: *"any deliberate approach by which school personnel, often in conjunction with parents and community members, help children and youth become caring, principled, and responsible. We do not use the term 'character education' to signify a particular philosophy, method, or program, as it has been used sometimes in the past. It is an umbrella term that encompasses diverse approaches and allows for many definitions/interpretations of 'character.'"*
>
> *"It is a planned effort by the whole community, through its institutions, to assist children and youth in becoming morally literate adults."* (DeRoche and Williams)
>
> *"It is an integral part of school life where the emphasis is on developing virtues—good habits and dispositions which lead students to responsible and mature adulthood."* (Ryan)
>
> *"It is education in civic virtue and in the qualities that teach children the forms and rules of citizenship in a just society and education in personal adjustment, chiefly the qualities that enable children to become productive and dependable citizens."* (London)
>
> *"It is helping young people develop a sense of social responsibility—that what they value matters and that living the virtues of responsibility, respect, self-discipline, integrity, and empathy lends meaning and richness to their own lives."* (Berreth and Berman)

The ultimate purpose of character education is to create schools that are caring, civil, and challenging and to develop young people who are smart, decent, and responsible.

6. Does character education really work?

If "working" means improving students' academic achievement, behaviors, attendance and truancy rates, school climate, and teacher morale, the answer is yes. If "working" means that students will become morally literate adults, practicing the values they learned at school, the answer is we do not know. There is little longitudinal data on the effects of character education efforts on youth behavior once they leave school. Even if we do not have a lot of empirical evidence about the payoff for character education, we believe that we should not let our children and youth learn personal and civic values by chance. We suspect that values learned, observed, and practiced in a positive, caring environment, both at home and at school, are more likely to stay with students throughout their lives.

EXPECTATIONS/OUTCOMES

Two key questions are:

1. What are the expectations of the stakeholders for the school's character education initiatives?
2. What outcomes do stakeholders anticipate?

The answers to these two questions will help inform stakeholders about the kind of character education initiatives that they want to create. The answers help with evaluation plans. Stakeholders who take the time, at this stage of the planning process, to articulate expectations for the program and delineate student outcomes have a greater likelihood of implementing a successful program. The value in reflecting on and recording expectations and outcomes is that they serve to drive the program and give focus to the evaluation process.

. . . schools should have high expectations for each and every student, and the education that students experience should reflect those expectations.

(French, 1998)[8]

Here is a checklist (chart 2.1) we recommend to help stakeholders determine what their expectations are for a character education program. The second step in determining expectations is to rephrase them as "outcomes." Once outcomes are established, you can begin gathering baseline data to ensure that the outcomes can be evaluated. The central question is: If your school is going to implement character education or already has a program, what are the stakeholders' expectations?

The checklist is just the beginning. By using it you can decide which expectations/outcomes are priorities for your school. Setting priorities may best be done by the Character Education Council (CEC), after the stakeholders have brainstormed the master list of expectations. As the CEC members refine the list, they can decide which expectations are most realistic and needed at the school.

Chart 2.1 Character Education Student Expectations/Outcomes

☐ better student behavior at school
☐ better student behavior in the home or community
☐ fewer classroom disruptions
☐ evidence that students have learned and are practicing the values taught
☐ examples of students respecting adults and each other
☐ more students doing their homework
☐ parents reporting positive behavior changes at home
☐ students demonstrating moral literacy in the cognitive, affective, and behavioral domains (thinking, feeling, doing)
☐ students developing and demonstrating a sense of efficacy and self-respect
☐ students demonstrating an understanding of multiple perspectives
☐ students demonstrating concern for the welfare of others
☐ students applying skills of moral reasoning and ethical decision making to solve problems
☐ students demonstrating skills of social cooperation
☐ students demonstrating responsibility for their own learning
☐ more students exhibiting a positive attitude toward learning, classwork, and school
☐ students contributing to the school's becoming more civil and compassionate

After the CEC completes its final list of expectations/outcomes for the school, its members need to examine some additional questions before continuing the process. Some key questions regarding outcomes are:

1. What percentage of students' successes in meeting the expectations, or reaching the outcomes, will be considered satisfactory?
2. Will your program demonstrate success if assessments show that student behaviors improve in school but there has been no impact on out-of-school behaviors?
3. Have the students been included in determining what their expectations are for the character education program?
4. Will the program be designed so that the outcomes have a good chance of being achieved over time?
5. What timelines have to be created to prepare stakeholders, especially school personnel and parents, for developing, planning, taking action, and identifying an appropriate program?

Setting expectations/outcomes is just one part of the planning process. Now, the fun begins—trying to get stakeholders to reach consensus on the values that are important to the school and community.

VALUES CONSENSUS

Clarity and agreement about the values your school and community want students to learn is essential. To be effective over the long term, congruent messages about values, behaviors, and expectations must permeate the home, school, and community. Consensus on values creates a coherent vision, which leads to a mission statement and an action plan for character education (see Tour Stop 3). In his research on effective schooling, Ed Wynne (1988)[10] identified this element as "coherence," calling it one of the single "best" indicators of school effectiveness.

Value consensus building can be a time-consuming and arduous task. Typical consensus-building activities require multiple meetings to brainstorm items and continue to whittle them down until stakeholders can agree to accept them. We have been using a values survey (VIP, chart 2.2) that we created to help groups get started with this process. By using the VIP, in sixty minutes a school/community group can have a basic set of core values upon which they all can agree.

Be sure that you invite representatives of parent and community groups to the consensus-building activity, along with school personnel (teachers, staff, administrators, and school board members). To get stakeholder buy-in, it is

Directions for the VIP Consensus Building: Three Steps

Step 1. Ask participants to choose five of the values on the list that they feel are important to them as people, and check these five values in the column on the left.

Step 2. Ask participants to choose five of the values on the list that they feel are important for children to learn in school (e.g., which values they want students to have by the time they graduate) and check those five values in the column on the right.

Step 3. Ask participants to get together in groups (no more than six people in a group) and, by merging the first two lists, try to come to consensus on a set of nine* values to teach in their school/community now.

[*Nine values is an arbitrary number; it can end up being six or even twelve.]

crucial to have people going through this consensus process together. During implementation, you will have little or no resistance to the program because stakeholders participated in the process of reaching consensus on the values to be taught at home, in school, and in the community.

As you can see, the VIP Survey is composed of a list of core values; some are specific and some are more global. We compiled this list from a variety of

Chart 2.2

V(values)   I(Identification)   P(Prioritization)

Column I	Values	Column II	Column III
Select 5 (you)		Select 5 (students)	Consensus (group)
_____	Self-discipline	_____	_____
_____	Patriotic	_____	_____
_____	Responsible	_____	_____
_____	Loyal	_____	_____
_____	Just	_____	_____
_____	Patient	_____	_____
_____	Compassionate	_____	_____
_____	Tolerant	_____	_____
_____	Ambitious	_____	_____
_____	Trustworthy	_____	_____
_____	Respectful	_____	_____
_____	Courteous	_____	_____
_____	Ethical	_____	_____
_____	Logical	_____	_____
_____	Courageous	_____	_____
_____	Loving	_____	_____
_____	Honest	_____	_____
_____	Caring	_____	_____
_____	Civic-minded	_____	_____
_____	Fair	_____	_____
_____	Perserverant	_____	_____
_____	Helpful	_____	_____
_____	Cooperative	_____	_____
_____	Forgiving	_____	_____
_____	other	_____	_____
_____	other	_____	_____

sources. The VIP is a survey that will help you generate a master list of values that are important for your school and community. We have found the VIP survey to be the least stressful and the quickest way to get the results you need.

VALUE DEFINITIONS

Participants in this experience will bring their own meaning to each of the values. The idea is to work with only those values about which there is common agreement. If it is one value, so be it. But our experience suggests that there will be common agreement, that is, more than a majority of the people in attendance will agree on at least six to twelve values on the list. These agreed-upon consensus values underscore the initial character education efforts. The tough task is to have stakeholders define them. We recommend that the Character Education Council do this, publicize the results, and request feedback. Pre-packaged definitions do not work; committees end up rejecting them and writing their own definitions. The benefits of taking the time to define terms are enormous, so plan on more than one meeting to define, distribute, get feedback, redefine, notify, and finalize definitions. The discussions alone are beneficial. As individuals share definitions for the values, their level of commitment to the program grows. The consensus-building process builds support, clarifies priorities, gains commitment, generates ideas for program activities, and helps to build a sense of community. It is important that the groups should not have to reinvent the wheel. Therefore, we suggest that you give them examples as they begin their discussions on values definitions (dictionaries can help).

To assist the CEC's work with defining values, we provide two examples of definitions for some of the core values that were chosen by a school district/community group (Character Plus program in Ferguson-Florissant, Missouri, *http://info.csd.org*).

VALUE	DEFINITION
Humanity	Believing that people of different cultures, abilities, religions, sexes, and races are equally valuable members of our society.
Respect	Showing regard for self, others, property, and those in authority.
Perseverance	Staying with a task; not giving up.
Service	Extending time and effort to help others.

Honesty	Being willing to say openly what is known to be true.
Responsibility	Being willing to be accountable for your own actions without blaming others.
Cooperation	Being able to work with others to accomplish a task.

Tempe Union High School District in Arizona (1996)

VALUE	DEFINITION
Honesty	Freedom from deceit or fraud.
Responsibility	Obligation, accountability, dependability for one's actions; to be answerable or accountable.
Compassion	A deep feeling for another, desire to remove another's misfortune.
Respect	Esteem for or a sense of the worth or excellence of self, others, property, and environment.
Integrity	Soundness of and adherence to moral principle and character.
Citizenship	The duties, rights, and privileges of the status of citizenship; a person's conduct as a citizen.
Service to Others	An act of giving assistance or advantage to another.

At this point in your plan of action, you and the CEC will have reviewed the answers to key questions about character and character education. There will be consensus on a set of core values and their meanings. Expectations and outcomes will have been identified. It is now time to examine some program standards that will guide the development of any action plan that you and the CEC design.

PROGRAM STANDARDS CHECKLIST

We include the program standards checklist (see chart 2.3)[11] as follows because many administrators find it to be a helpful planning guide in starting a character education program. The intent of the checklist is to help you and others make thoughtful decisions about comprehensive program planning, implementation, and evaluation.

Chart 2.3   Character Education Program Standards Checklist

A well-planned Comprehensive Character Education Program:

- ☐ is organized to educate and support the efforts of parents/guardians in value formation;
- ☐ includes a mission statement and a clear set of program expectations and outcomes;
- ☐ is implemented after the comprehensive program is aligned with the school or the district's mission and goals;
- ☐ is implemented after the need for the program is established and made public;
- ☐ is implemented after the stakeholders have agreed to the values that will underpin the program;
- ☐ has an organizational structure (Character Education Council) that is responsible for implementing the framework and addressing the standards;
- ☐ provides opportunities for meaningful involvement of parents, school personnel, and community members;
- ☐ establishes and sustains school and classroom climates that foster the core values;
- ☐ has resources available to carry out all aspects of the program;
- ☐ provides ongoing staff development and other support services;
- ☐ involves all stakeholders in ongoing evaluation plans;
- ☐ utilizes the resources of the district's central office and the community;
- ☐ is designed to improve the quality of school life for students, their families, and all school personnel;
- ☐ is designed to build strong, long-lasting relationships between home, school, and the community; and
- ☐ contributes to the development of positive personal, prosocial, and civic values in the students in its program(s).

Intelligence plus character—that is the goal of true education.
—Martin Luther King, Jr.

TOUR THOUGHTS

Here is what we said in 1998, in the first edition of *Hearts and Minds*.

> School and community agencies should help parents provide children and youth with a moral road map or compass. The "moral compass" will help direct children and youth along a route to living a life based on moral principles. At times, some will leave the highway taking various routes, trying new roads, testing unmarked ways, and taking turnoffs. The moral road map will be highlighted by warning signs, stoplights, caution markers, and bulletin boards describing the risks when deviating from the main route. However, there will always be internal and external detectors (guidance from one's conscience and from others) along the route. There will always be stations where one can stop for directions on how to get back to the "moral highway."[12]

Given the events in many schools (killings, violence, bullying, harassment, etc.) since we wrote this passage, we are more convinced than ever that schools and communities across this nation must get actively involved in the character development of young people. The next tour stop deals with the leadership necessary to do just that.

JEFFERSON JUNIOR HIGH SCHOOL, WASHINGTON, DC

Our tour bus rounds the corner heading toward Jefferson Junior High School, not far from the Mall in Washington, DC.[13] Each of us is given an advertisement from the *New York Times* (September 28, 1997) that highlights the four winners of the Harold W. McGraw, Jr. Prize in Education. We read the following:

> *Vera M. White—Achievement through Character Education*
> As principal of Jefferson Junior High School in the heart of Washington, DC's inner-city, Vera White has made character education and high expectations into powerful vehicles for achievement in her minority student body. Through this deliberate effort to teach right and wrong through good example, curriculum, and total school environment, she has harnessed the resources of all members of her school

community to help all students discover, and believe, that they can succeed in whatever they wish to accomplish.

Ms. White, a tall, energetic woman, meets us at the school entrance. One of the first things we notice is that the metal detector is in the corner of the hallway, unused. Ms. White lets the group know that she sees it as an insult to the staff, students, and parents of the school.

As we tour the school, we are told about the rigorous academic program and high expectations for achievement. Coupled with high academic requirements is an emphasis on character development. Every morning, we are told, students spend an hour in their homerooms working with teachers on their self-esteem, confidence, manners, and other values, such as respect and responsibility, all designed to foster the character development of students at the school. Ms. White tells us that the character education program was implemented five years ago to confront students with their irresponsible behaviors. Students have learned lessons in conflict avoidance and resolution. They are learning to take responsibility for their bodies and behaviors. Students are focused and they are attending school, making Jefferson the only school in the city with perfect attendance.

Ms. White shares stories with us about how hard she works to form "partnerships" with the community, government agencies, and local companies. These partnerships have helped with grants for new laboratories, computers, and instructional materials.

The success of the school, we are told, can be found in discussions with students and parents. But one telling fact is that of the 800 students, about one-third are not from the neighborhood but from other areas of the city, both poor and wealthy. There is a waiting list of over 500 students.

As we leave the school, we are serenaded by the students as they sing "I Believe I Can Fly," and they wave good-bye to us.

E. F. DeRoche and M. M. Williams, *Educating Hearts and Minds: A Comprehensive Character Education Framework,* 2d ed. (Thousand Oaks, CA: Corwin Press, 2001), chaps. 2 and 3.

H. A. Huffman, *Developing a Character Education Program: One School District's Experience* (Alexandria, VA: Association for Supervision and Curriculum Development, 1994).

T. Lickona, *Educating for Character: Teaching Respect and Responsibility* (New York: Bantam Books, 1991).

Center for the Fourth and Fifth R's (Respect/Responsibility), *http://www.cortland.edu/www/c4n5rs*.

Character Plus [formerly—PREP], *http://info.csd.org/staffdev/chared/character plus.html*.

Communitarian Network, *http://www.gwu.edu/~ccps*.

REFERENCES

1. S. Elam and L. Rose, The 27th annual Phi Delta Kappan/Gallup Poll of the public's attitudes toward the public schools. *Phi Delta Kappan* 76, no. 1 (1995): 41–56.
2. J. Kauffman and H. Burbach, "On Creating a Climate of Classroom Civility." *Phi Delta Kappan* 74, no. 4: 324.
3. M. Talbot and N. Tate, "Shared Values in a Pluralist Society?" In R. Smith and P. Standish, eds., *Teaching Right and Wrong: Moral Education in the Balance* (London, Great Britain: Cromwell Press Ltd., 1997), 1–14.
4. B. D. Brooks, *The Case for Character Education* (Northridge, CA: Studio 4 Productions, 1997), 28.
5. J. Dalton and M. Watson, *Among Friends: Classrooms Where Caring and Learning Prevail* (Oakland, CA: Developmental Studies Center, 1997), 35.
6. T. Sizer and N. Sizer, *The Children Are Watching: Schools and the Moral Contract* (Boston, MA: Beacon Press, 1999).
7. M. M. Williams and E. Schaps, eds., *Character Education: The Foundation for Teacher Education,* The Report of the ATE National Commission on Character Education, (Washington, DC: Character Education Partnership, 1999).
8. D. French, "The State's Role in Shaping a Progressive Vision of Public Education." *Phi Delta Kappan* 80, no. 3 (1998): 193.
9. E. Wynne, "A Good School." In K. Ryan and J. Cooper, eds., *Kaleidoscope: Readings in Education* (Boston: Houghton-Mifflin, 1988).
10. Adapted from E. F. DeRoche, and M. M. Williams, *Educating Hearts and Minds: A Comprehensive Character Education Framework,* 2d ed. (Thousand Oaks, CA: Corwin Press, 2001).
11. E. F. DeRoche and M. M. Williams, *Educating Hearts and Minds: A Comprehensive Character Education Framework* (Thousand Oaks, CA: Corwin Press, 1998), 24.
12. This story comes from Michael Janofsky's article "A Bright Light in a City Shadowed by Trouble," which appeared in the *New York Times,* September 28, 1997, 10.

• *Tour Stop 3* •

Leadership

A leader is a dealer in hope.

—Napoleon Bonaparte

There are as many books on leadership as there are travel guides. To narrow the leadership field to one chapter requires a very specific focus. That focus is captured in the question: What is required of you, as the school principal, to create and maintain effective, successful, and comprehensive character education initiatives in your school?

You are the school's leader. Your job as principal is to lead, manage, serve, and evaluate. You are the school's tour guide. You are the one driving the school bus, looking out the front window to the future and checking the rear-view mirror to see where you have been. As you drive the bus, ask yourself these questions:

- Who knows the school better than you do?
- Who has the best opportunity to help the staff and others develop the school's character education program?
- Who is in the best position to get the resources the CEC will need?
- Who has the primary responsibility to set the vision and mission for the program?
- Who has the best opportunity to interpret and explain the school's character education efforts to the stakeholders, the public, and the media?
- Who is in the best position to encourage others to take leadership responsibilities for the school's character education initiatives?

- Who will adults and students look to as examples of people modeling the values underpinning the school's character education efforts?
- Who is in the best position to change school policies and procedures to conform to the principles that underscore the program?
- Who is the main person responsible for the school's climate?
- Who is in the best position to ensure that students and parents are on the same character education tour bus?

Are you convinced? We are! It is you! So here is some advice.

To drive the school's character education program, you will have to play many roles. We highlight nine of them here.

VISIONARY

There is no more powerful engine driving an organization toward excellence and long-range success than an attractive, worthwhile, and achievable vision of the future, widely shared.

(Nanus, 1992)[1]

You need a vision of what your school's character education program can be—its potential. What are its possibilities? Your vision should encompass the ideal for students—what they can become academically, morally, socially, and behaviorally.

> Have a vision—share it!
> Have a vision—use it!
> Have a vision—plan it!

Hoover (1998) advises that this century's school principal must take charge, do what is right, seek improvements, network with peers, focus on the teacher, and strive for emotional and physical health.

MISSIONARY

"... *The foundation of an effective organization (is) its mission and values.*"

(Blanchard and O'Connor, 1997)[2]

Leadership   33

If the character education initiatives are going to "take hold" in your school, it will be because you are its missionary; you are the message-carrier to the flock. Your zeal for the program will show as you articulate and communicate the program's mission and goals.

The mission should be clear, concise, cogent, and in writing. It should tell what the school is about, what it stands for, what it believes, what principles it adopts. Here is an example from a school district, a high school, and an elementary school:

Clayton School District, Missouri

> The district's mission is to strive to develop in all its children the strength of character, the skills, the knowledge, and the wisdom necessary to build creative, productive lives and contribute to a global society.

Mountain Pointe High School
Tempe Union High School District, Tempe, Arizona

> The purpose of our community is to ensure a safe, supportive learning environment which empowers all students to realize their potential by accepting responsibility for active civic involvement, by displaying pride in oneself and for others, and by demonstrating high levels of academic performance.

Regnart Elementary School, Cupertino, CA (M. Murphy, 1998)[3]

> The stages of character development can be compared to that of a flower. It begins with a tightly folded bud and then with the nurturing of the sun, water, and soil, it blossoms into a cluster of petals. Each petal of that flower represents a different aspect in a child's character development: honesty, integrity, responsibility, consideration of others, respect for self.

The principal as moral agent must address *"the issues of values in education and recognize the moral dimensions of schooling. The principal's school activities are intertwined with critical ethical issues, (and the position) is being slowly transformed into an instrument of social justice."*

(J. Murphy, 1998)[4]

Goals put the mission of the character education efforts "on the road." Goals are the expectations of the stakeholders. Goals are the "routes" you and others take on the journey. Goals give direction. They tell you what training and resources you will need. Goals inform program implementation. But, most important, goals help set the standards and intended outcomes of the program.

Simply put, what are the goals of your school's character education efforts? There are two ways to answer this question. One way is to identify overall program goals, such as:

- ☑ To make this school a caring, civil, safe, and challenging place to teach and learn.
- ☑ To implement, in the daily life of the school, the core values of the character education program.
- ☑ To integrate the character education program into the curriculum.

Another way you might address goals is to do so by types of goals—for example:

- ☑ Process goals: The committees will effectively guide the school's character education efforts.
- ☑ Staff goals: The staff will assume ownership of the program and model the core values.
- ☑ Program goals: The program will be integrated into the curriculum and the daily life of the school.
- ☑ Student goals: The students will actively participate in the program and will learn and practice the core values of the program.

The role of the principal, your role, is to keep the goals on the agenda of committees and before all stakeholders so that they see you setting a priority for the school's character education program. Therefore, you are the goaltender, and, as you will see, goals also inform standards and assessment.

A study of school reform conducted by the Consortium on Renewing Education[5] found that high-performing schools were those with "stable leadership" and a "no-nonsense, unapologetic intention to influence student values." These two factors were coupled with an "authoritative stance towards attendance, decorum, and expectations." In these schools, the focus was on teaching and learning, on linking student experiences with student learning, and on responding to failing, at-risk students. Note the key words in this quote that apply to a school's character education program: leadership, expectations, values, decorum, attendance, meaningful learning, and student experiences.

STANDARD BEARER

"Successful leaders of the twenty-first century will be those who give followers what they need, when they need it, in a form in which they can use it."

(Beck and Yeager, 1994)[6]

Education is inundated (maybe drowning) with standards. Students, teachers, and administrators are faced with performance standards, academic (testing) standards, subject matter standards, graduation standards, and so on. So, why should character education be any different?

Your school's character education mission and goals are best guided by standards. Since you carry the "banner" as the standard bearer for your school's program, we offer a definition and an example.

A standard may be considered a statement of quality or value that can be used to guide and judge the effectiveness of program implementation, maintenance, and evaluation. You should help stakeholders develop a standard-driven character education program. To help you do this, we have developed character education program standards, curriculum standards, partnership standards, teaching standards, and assessment standards, which should be used as part of a comprehensive framework for character education initiatives.[7] Each chapter in this book has checklists, statements, or questions that represent standards for each of the framework's components.

The Character Education Partnership (see page 4) offers eleven principles, which we will call standards, to be used to guide and evaluate character education efforts. A summary of these "standards" follows (*www.character.org*):

- ☑ The basis of good character is the core ethical values and is defined to include thinking, feeling, and behavior.
- ☑ Effective character education programs are comprehensive, intentional, and proactive.
- ☑ Effective character education programs require moral leadership from stakeholders.
- ☑ Effective character education programs are a complement to and integrated with an academic program that is challenging, meaningful, engaging, and intrinsically motivating for all students.

- ☑ Effective character education programs must assess the character of the school, the growth of the staff as character educators, and students' character and behaviors.
- ☑ The school must be a caring community, providing students with opportunities to learn and practice moral action and leadership.
- ☑ The school staff, as well as parents and community members, must form meaningful partnerships, foster and support the program's core values, and engage in opportunities to share responsibilities as a learning and moral community.

Principals *"will need to design and construct an integrated network of social agencies—possibly with the school at the hub—to address the conditions confronting many students and their families."*

(J. Murphy, 1998)[8]

ARCHITECT

The foundation of your school's character education efforts is constructed around the "mission" cornerstone. The foundation consists of the goals and objectives of the program. The foundation must include input from all the stakeholders, from the school bus driver to people at the central office. The foundation is built upon the vision and mission, on the goals and objectives, on standards and partnerships, and on resources and assessment. Your skill in designing a carefully constructed plan is essential at the beginning stages of the program.

The following checklist poses questions by former assistant superintendent and current director of the Character Education Institute at California University of Pennsylvania, Henry Huffman,[9] to help you get off to a successful start and carry out your role as the architect of your school's program.

Huffman's Process Checklist

- ☐ What is the readiness of the community for a character education program?
- ☐ Have stakeholders and community leaders been identified and involved in the planning?
- ☐ Has a proactive communications process been initiated that informs stakeholders of what comprehensive character education is,

why schools have a role to play, and how schools intentionally seek to influence moral development?
- ☐ Has the planning group developed a common character education knowledge base and vocabulary that will allow it to make informed decisions about the specifics of the initiative?
- ☐ Has the planning group agreed on ground rules for its work?
- ☐ Has the community identified a set of moral values that it wants its schools to give increased attention to in all aspects of its operation?
- ☐ Have action plans been developed for implementing a comprehensive character education initiative?
- ☐ Has an evaluation plan been developed for the initiative?
- ☐ Has the school board made a public commitment to the initiative?
- ☐ Has a structure been developed for nurturing the initiative over the long term?

Murphy and Lewis (1994)[10] *attribute success of school reform endeavors (and character education is certainly one) to the principal's direct efforts to model and reinforce behaviors related to the common vision and shared values.*

EDUCATOR

Your role as educator is captured in such words as *teacher* and *coach, encourager* and *empowerer, mentor* and *model, collaborator* and *supporter.*

- ☑ As educator, you must model the values of the program, for others will bear witness to your words and actions.
- ☑ As educator, you must help others learn and practice the agreed-upon values.
- ☑ As educator, you must teach others about the moral/character dimensions of education at your school.
- ☑ As educator, you must engage others to collaborate, to network, to team, to share power and status, and to assume responsibilities.
- ☑ As educator, you must be eager to learn, willing to self-evaluate, be open to feedback, engage in discussions and debates, and be a good listener.
- ☑ As educator, you must work to create a sense in your school that all are there as a community of learners, helping each other learn and change, and helping each other care and share.

☑ As educator, you must tell the stories about the school, both past (traditions) and present. You must explain the rules and procedures. You must share with others the values that underscore the school's character education program.

COMMUNICATOR

The effective principal is a communication center for the education hub . . . guiding the development of learning efforts for knowledge workers.

(Achilles, Keedy, and High, in L. Hughes, *The Principal as Leader,* 1999)[11]

Understatements: One, you cannot do it by yourself. Two, the school cannot do character education alone. Three, you need to communicate with others.

Essential Requirement: Effective communication with all of the stakeholders and with those who express interest in the program, and especially people who question the program.

Lesson: From Henry Huffman, the former assistant superintendent for instruction in the Mt. Lebanon School District (Pittsburgh), who has been through the process of initiating a character education program. His commentary on communication is instructive.

Huffman[12] highlights the importance of developing a communication plan. Although he says little about the role of the school principal, his suggestions to make presentations about the program to all employees, to community groups, to parents, and to students are important. He also emphasizes the importance of written communication that includes:

- the efforts that went into the need for the program;
- mission and goals statements;
- parameters and strategies;
- action plans;
- definition of terms;
- a summary of schools of thought on educating for character; and
- descriptions of other programs, as well as of resources and references.

Huffman[13] also describes four lessons learned from his experiences creating and implementing a district-wide character education program. Following are his four lessons, which should be helpful to you:

Lesson 1: Written communication by itself is inadequate. The character education leader must get out into the community to explain and promote the program. The principal must communicate with all school employees and keep the mission and goals of the program on the yearly school agenda. Since parental support is crucial, Huffman recommends that they be helped to understand the purpose of the program, the methodologies to be used to deliver the program, how they can help, and what evaluation procedures will be used.

Lesson 2: Do not neglect to communicate with classified personnel about all aspects of the program. In this communication, provide opportunities for employees to express their concerns, try to answer their questions, and offer them opportunities to participate.

Lesson 3: Give priority to character education. Do not let some of the stakeholders assume the attitude that "this too will pass," as just another of many school reform efforts.

Lesson 4: Attend to the critics of the program in a way that models the very values the school's character education program fosters; that is, respect, responsibility, honesty, and integrity.

If you have already begun character education initiatives at your school, we have put together a communication ideas checklist you should find very helpful.

Communication Ideas Checklist

- ☐ Hold informal sessions with stakeholders.
- ☐ Hold breakfasts, luncheons, or receptions with small representative groups of teachers, staff, parents, students, and community leaders.
- ☐ Meet the media, invite them to the school, and have them meet the teachers and students.
- ☐ Prepare a video on some of the ways the teachers and students are fostering the values of the program, make copies of the video, and distribute them to parents and the public.
- ☐ Have the staff and students write and videotape success stories about the program for the media and others.
- ☐ Meet at least once a month with all the classified personnel in your school to exchange information and answer questions.
- ☐ Develop a strong student council that is media- and communication-conscious.
- ☐ Meet with parents; communicate with parents; get parents involved; develop parent programs; and when you think you have done enough with the parents—do more.

☐ Form partnerships with businesses, with senior citizens, and with people in the community around the school.

 A good principal ... *"communicates the school's mission clearly and consistently to staff members, parents, and students."*

(Keller, 1998)[14]

A good principal, according to current thinking, has the following leadership characteristics:[15]

- ☑ Recognizes *teaching and learning* as the main businesses of a school;
- ☑ *Communicates* the school's mission clearly and consistently to staff members, parents, and students;
- ☑ Fosters *standards* for teaching and learning that are high and attainable;
- ☑ Provides clear *goals* and *monitors* the progress of students toward meeting them;
- ☑ Spends *time* in classrooms and *listens* to teachers and students;
- ☑ Promotes an *atmosphere* of trust and sharing;
- ☑ Builds a good staff and makes *professional development* a primary concern; and
- ☑ Does not tolerate bad teachers.

PROVIDER

 *"When teachers need things, the principal delivers. Resources are anything the principal can use to satisfy teacher needs: materials, student discipline, insulating teachers from parents, organizational maintenance. . . . (Being a) resource provider may have the most potential for developing teacher leadership."*[16]

(Achilles, Keedy, and High, 1998)

Let us get to the point here: the principal is the school's resource provider. A character education program needs resources, both fiscal and human. The program needs resources for materials, for student activities, for parent education, for release time for staff, for efforts to form partnerships, and for program evaluation. But most important, the program needs resources for staff development. There are at least six purposes for staff development. These purposes can be used to map staff-development opportunities.

Six Purposes

1. To improve, enhance, and deepen the staff's knowledge and understanding of character education and the moral development of children and youth.
2. To contribute to the skills and abilities of teachers to incorporate the core values into the curriculum.
3. To foster among the staff members positive attitudes and confidence that they can influence a student's moral and social development.
4. To enhance morale among the staff members and encourage them to continually look for better teaching methods.
5. To provide the staff members with the opportunity to share their study, their work, their ideas, their experiences, their projects, and their sense of what works and what does not work.
6. To enable the staff to spend time discussing the curriculum and school-wide activities, which underpin the school's character education initiatives.

Ideas for staff development opportunities follow:

Mapping Staff-Development Opportunities

- ☐ mini-sabbaticals
- ☐ work-study groups
- ☐ interaction with consultants
- ☐ seminars and workshops
- ☐ academies, institutes, and conferences
- ☐ college courses
- ☐ online courses
- ☐ self-study
- ☐ school visitations
- ☐ classroom observations
- ☐ summer projects
- ☐ action research
- ☐ reading clubs
- ☐ add your ideas_____

Staff development is treated more fully at Tour Stop 6.

EVALUATOR

 *"Are you planning to do the evaluation work yourself? If so, remember two things: (1) it will take some time and resources; and (2) you are likely to be somewhat biased about the work being evaluated."*

(Berkowitz, 1998)[17]

At Tour Stop 9, we discuss things principals do when evaluating a school's character education efforts. Here we will simply reemphasize what you already know; the "results buck" stops at your desk. You are the responsible person for evaluating the school's programs and the personnel who deliver them. At some point, stakeholders will want to know about the outcomes, the results, and the "payoff" for the school's character education initiatives. The evaluation process should continually accompany you and others on the character education journey. While part of it may occur when the journey is over (summative evaluation), which it never will be, most of the evaluation efforts should occur along the road as the program is planned and implemented (formative evaluation).

Your role is to create an environment where evaluation and feedback are both appreciated and understood. Your role continues to be that of an educator—helping stakeholders to find effective ways to assess the program. Your role as architect is to help them organize and plan for evaluation. Your responsibility is to ensure that they are focusing on the goals and expectations of the program as they create evaluation plans. Your advice will be that they create "benchmarks" along the way and that they use a variety of evaluative methods, not just those that reflect "number crunching" but also those that provide rich descriptions of what the teachers and students are doing. Your counsel will encourage them to ask meaningful and penetrating questions about what they are doing and why they are doing it. This will enable them to be critical thinkers and reflectors of their actions and each component of the program and activities.

Here are some "principles for principals" that can be used to evaluate your school's character education program:

- Keep the focus on goals and expectations.
- Emphasize the importance of ongoing, continuous evaluation.
- Make it a team effort involving as many stakeholders as possible.

- Stress the positive aspects of evaluation.
- Provide the training that personnel will need for evaluative purposes.
- Highlight the value of self-evaluation.
- Encourage the reflection on and discussion of findings.
- Ensure that evaluation contributes to program and behavior changes.
- Ensure that the process is open, honest, and free from threats.
- Encourage the stakeholders to use results for short- and long-term planning.
- Ensure that evaluative results are communicated clearly and effectively to all parties.

TOUR THOUGHT

We do not have to tell you that it is not easy being a school leader. At this tour stop we discussed the many tasks to be performed by a principal. In fact, we wonder how you do it. But it is getting done. It may take your time and your patience and certainly a lot of your energy, but it seems to us that principals are working diligently to meet the demands placed upon them as the school leaders. In addition to all the previously mentioned tasks you are faced with, the public is interested in test results. Led by the press and legislators, your school and others are being evaluated not on a range of qualities but on one factor—test scores. So, the question from one principal in a workshop is appreciated. He asked: "Will character education improve test scores of the kids in my school?" This is not an idle question. The answer is important. The evidence suggests that it will.

LEWENBERG MIDDLE SCHOOL

If it is Tuesday, it must be Boston! (O'Donnell, 1997)[19] Our tour bus pulls into the parking lot of the Solomon Lewenberg Middle School. We are about to enter a school that survived because of the leadership of its principal. The wonderful story we will hear is about changing a school climate. It is about people who demonstrate that leadership, persistence, and involvement really count.

Before we meet the former principal of the school, Thomas O'Neill, we are greeted by Mark O'Donnell, who provides us with some history about this middle school. He tells us about the conditions of the school prior to 1984. He describes a neglected school in a neglected neighborhood. We hear that as white residents moved out of the area, minority families moved in, and the school board and central office paid little attention to the school. The school grounds, he says, were a haven for muggers and a junkyard for the neighborhood. Inside the school, enrollment declined as test scores declined. He tells us about the discipline problems and lack of support from parents; about the perception of the school being an unsafe environment for children, causing the school board to consider closing the school and sending the 300 students to "safer" schools.

We are introduced to Thomas O'Neill, a fourteen-year veteran of the public schools who was principal of Lewenberg from 1984 to 1994. He tells us that in 1984, when he was asked to be the school principal, he knew it would be a major leadership challenge. He accepted the responsibility. Along with the support from his staff and some parents, one of the first things he had to do, he said, was to clean up the grounds. Volunteers dedicated many weekends to the project and the school grounds were cleaned and trees planted, which were purchased as a result of parent/teacher group fundraising drives. Mr. O'Neill says that evidently the cleaning of the grounds and planting of trees angered the custodian union, and the trees and other bushes were pulled up. He told the union that he and his group would plant "two trees for every one you pull up." He says that he had been at odds with the district's maintenance department over the care of the inside and outside of the building and that he and his family endured threats of physical harm. Yet, the relationships he nurtured with the custodians assigned to the school during his principalship eventually resulted in a warm, attractive, clean, and bright school.

He takes our tour group through the main entrance of the school, where there is a reading and study area for students. As we walk through the school, with its wide corridors and its classic high ceilings so prominent in schools built in the early 1900s, Principal O'Neill shows us the attractive kitchen and small cafeteria built by volunteers using materials donated by local merchants. He tells us that the student council runs the cafeteria and proceeds are used to fund field trips. One of our tour members comments about the fact that all classroom doors are open and that groups of students are working with one another and the teacher. Since our group got "caught" in the corridor when classes were changing, more than one member commented about the orderly, quiet, and mature ways students were changing classes.

He takes the group into an empty classroom to show us a copy of the "Full Value Contract," which appears in every classroom. It is a list of "agreements" that students and staff members are expected to uphold everyday. He says that he and the staff set high expectations for all students; that they emphasize the point that "no one can make it alone;" and that they believe in "hands-on learning—you learn by doing." Students are taught how to work together and how to pool their resources, skills, and talents to solve problems.

He shows the group the gym whose walls were once covered with graffiti but that now display bright, colorful outdoor scenes painted by the school's art teacher. One of the first things we note about the gym is the climbing stations that have been built around it. With pride, he introduces us to three teachers who created "Project Adventure," a *Reader's Digest* award–winning physical education program that involves all students in a five-day-a-week for six weeks intense physical training course that teaches students advanced climbing skills and much more. The staff feels that the continuing steady gains in academic achievement and student behaviors are a result of Project Adventure, the high expectations they have for students, and the emphasis on group learning strategies.

Mark O'Donnell leads us back to the tour bus, saying that while the area continues to be a "struggling urban neighborhood," the school has changed and students in the school want to be successful. He tells us that Tom O'Neill left the school in 1994 to accept another challenging position as principal of a suburban middle school.

We thank him for arranging this tour stop. As we quietly sit on the bus and reflect on this experience, we hear talk about leadership, change, the plight of urban schools, and the importance of school climate.

S. R. Covey, *Principle Centered Leadership* (New York, NY: Simon and Schuster, 1991).

W. Glasser, *The Quality School: Managing Students without Coercion* (New York, NY: HarperCollins, 1992).

Journal of Leadership Studies JournalLeadership_Journal@baker.edu.

K. Peterson and T. Deal, "How Leaders Influence the Culture of Schools." *Educational Leadership* 56, no. 1 (1998): 28–30.

T. J. Sergiovanni, *Moral Leadership: Getting to the Heart of School Improvement* (San Francisco, CA: Jossey-Bass, 1992).

R. J. Starratt, *Transforming Educational Administration: Meaning, Community, and Excellence* (New York, NY: McGraw-Hill, 1996).

American Association of School Administrators, *http://www.aasa.org*.
The Center for Collaborative Education: An Affiliate of the Coalition of Essential Schools, *http://www.cce.org*.
Community of Caring, *http://www.communityofcaring.org*.
Josephson Institute of Ethics, "Character Counts! Coalition," *www.charactercounts.org/ccwelcome.htm*.

REFERENCES

1. B. Nanus, *Visionary Leadership* (San Francisco, CA: Jossey-Bass, 1992), 3.

2. K. Blanchard and M. O'Connor, *Managing by Values* (San Francisco, CA: Berrett-Koehler, 1997), 3.

3. M. Murphy, *Character Education in America's Blue Ribbon Schools* (Lancaster, PA: Technomic, 1998), 55.

4. J. Murphy, "What's Ahead for Tomorrow's Principals?" *Principal* 78, no. 1 (September 1998): 16.

5. Consortium on Renewing Education, "Forum." *Education Week* 18, no. 12 (December 1998): 24.

6. D. Beck and N. Yeager, *The Leader's Window: Mastering the Four Styles of Leadership to Build High-Performing Teams* (New York, NY: John Wiley & Sons, 1994), 7.

7. E. F. DeRoche and M. M. Williams, *Educating Hearts and Minds: A Comprehensive Character Education Framework,* 2d ed. (Thousand Oaks, CA: Corwin Press, 2001).

8. J. Murphy, "What's Ahead for Tomorrow's Principals?" *Principal* 78, no. 1 (September 1998): 16.

9. H. Huffman, correspondence.

10. J. Murphy and L. Lewis, *Reshaping the Principalship: Insights from Transformational Reform Efforts* (Thousand Oaks, CA: Corwin Press, 1994), 1.

11. C. Achilles, J. Keedy, and R. High, "The Political World of the Principal: How Principals Get Things Done." In L. Hughes, ed., *The Principal as Leader* (New York, NY: Macmillan College Publishing, 1998), 43.

12. H. Huffman, *Developing a Character Education Program: One School District's Experience* (Alexandria, VA: Association for Supervision and Curriculum Development, 1994), chap. 3.

13. H. Huffman, *Developing a Character Education Program: One School District's Experience* (Alexandria, VA: Association for Supervision and Curriculum Development, 1994), 26–30.

14. B. Keller, "Principal Matters." *Education Week* 18, no. 11 (November 1998): 26.

15. B. Keller, "Principal Matters." *Education Week* 18, no. 11 (November 1998): Leadership Characteristics.

16. C. Achilles, J. Keedy, and R. High, "The Political World of the Principal: How Principals Get Things Done." In L. Hughes, ed., *The Principal as Leader* (New York, NY: Macmillan College, 1998), 39.

17. M. Berkowitz, *A Primer for Evaluating a Character Education Initiative* (Washington, DC: The Character Education Partnership, 1998), 7.

18. M. O'Donnell, "Boston's Lewenberg Middle School Delivers Success." *Phi Delta Kappan* 78, no. 7 (1997): 508–512.

• *Tour Stop 4* •

School Climate

> *One of the nicest things about character education . . . is that it improves teacher morale, thereby almost immediately changing the climate of the school.*
>
> —Gordon Vessels, unpublished manuscript

Whether you call it culture or climate, no character education program is going to be successful without a supporting and nurturing environment that is caring, civil, and challenging, both academically and behaviorally.

Climate is a mosaic of elements that identifies the school's "personality." School climate is the incubator for value formation, for character development, and for academic achievement. Each school, even within the same school district, has its own unique school climate.

We are reminded of the opening scene of the film *Dead Poets' Society*, in which the students are marching into the school assembly carrying banners that expressed the "four pillars" of Welton Academy: *Tradition—Excellence—Discipline—Honor*. If they actually get played out in the day-to-day activities of the academy, then these "pillars" help form this school's climate.

A school's climate embodies a host of factors that are captured in such words as expectations, modeling, service, relationships, and appearances. It requires close attention to where the students are and what they do when they are in classrooms and labs, in the gym or on the field, on field trips or at athletic events, in the hallways or in study halls, on the playground or in the cafeteria, in the library or in the media center, in the parking lot or on the school bus.

Lunenburg and Ornstein[1] point out that schools that demonstrate a positive climate have, among other factors, principals who expect the best from their teachers, get the resources teachers need to do their job, have influence with their supervisors, support teachers, and protect teachers from outside forces that may be unreasonable, threatening, or hostile.

As the saying goes,
"Accent-u-ate the positive!
E-lim-in-ate the negative!"

ROLES AND RESPONSIBILITIES

The principal's roles that we described at Tour Stop 3 play out in promoting and maintaining a positive school climate. Thus, we can see that, as principal, you are the school's cultural architect. You must communicate with and educate the stakeholders to better understand the interrelationships between the school's climate, the character education initiatives, academic achievement, and the socio-emotional behaviors of students. You are the builder of cultural elements such as rituals, ceremonies, and traditions. As educator, your role is to advise and counsel students and others about the influence that subcultures (peer groups, cliques, gangs, clubs, sport groups) have on school climate. This is particularly necessary in middle and secondary schools. As evaluator, your role is to construct ways to evaluate the climate of your school.

We like Deal and Peterson's[2] construction of five key roles that principals play in shaping a school's culture. We have modified their idea somewhat, but, in general, they believe that a principal acts as a:

1. *Symbol*—The school's core values are fostered by creating a view of what the school "should and could be" and what it stands for, by the way the principal dresses, by his/her daily behaviors and routine activities, by his/her attention to events, by his/her appreciation of school activities, and by his/her communication of beliefs about instruction.
2. *Potter*—The culture (core values) of the school is shaped by the way the principal "molds" into the mix the school's heroes and heroines, traditions and rituals, ceremonies and celebrations, rituals and routines, and, of course, by hiring teachers and staff who support the core values of the school.

3. *Poet*—The school culture is enhanced by the way the principal communicates, orally and in writing, the values, beliefs, ideas, and core values. Promoting the "language" of character, the use of metaphors, the telling of stories, and "painting images" of the school and its values are a few of the ways a principal serves as poet.
4. *Actor*—A principal plays many roles with an ever-changing daily script. Improvisation is a skill that is useful in meeting the dramas, comedies, and tragedies that occur in the daily life of the school. But as an actor responding to changing scenes and untested scripts, the principal seeks opportunities to communicate, reinforce, and nurture the values and beliefs that make for a positive and enriching school climate.
5. *Healer*—A principal advances the school culture by ministering to individuals and groups when they have a need to cope with loss or hurt, isolation or indifference, or events that tear at the fabric of the school as a community and family.

Strong positive cultures are places with a shared sense of what is important, a shared ethos of caring and concern, and a shared commitment to helping students learn . . . Without the attention of leaders, school cultures can become toxic and unproductive. By paying fervent attention to the symbolic side of their schools, leaders can help develop the foundation for change and success.

(Peterson and Deal, 1999)[3]

FIFTY WAYS TO IMPROVE YOUR SCHOOL'S CLIMATE

When planning to improve the climate of the school and the content of the character education program, you and others should consider the following fifty ideas.

1. Integrate the core values into the curriculum, programs, and activities.
2. Develop posters, pictures, banners, and bulletin boards that promote the core values.
3. Establish regular recognition ceremonies and celebrations of student successes.
4. Offer character education assemblies for the students, staff, and parents.

5. Develop violence-prevention and safety-education programs.
6. Flexible Fridays: Students have an opportunity to engage in a variety of mini-courses and activities; some may be student-planned and implemented.
7. Hold a yearly character-education parade.
8. Kudos Boxes for students and staff. Cards are filled out by anyone at the school. Each card says: "I think _____ deserves kudos because . . ."
9. Celebrate holidays and famous peoples' birthdays.
10. Develop partnerships and mentoring programs.
11. Have fairs and arts and crafts programs that show off the students' work.
12. Create service-learning projects for the school, home, and community.
13. Consider cross-age tutoring programs.
14. Create a school student-leadership program.
15. Develop partnerships with local businesses, agencies, and organizations.
16. Have programs that recognize student achievements in sports and academics.
17. Promote the use of civil and polite language in the school.
18. Have guest speakers and celebrities in classes and at assemblies who can address the values of the school or tell stories that examine the human experience.
19. Encourage student participation in patriotic and citizenship activities.
20. Develop family-involvement programs and activities.
21. Involve students in school rule making.
22. Create after-school, special weekend, and/or summer programs that are designed to meet student remedial and enrichment needs.
23. Create a student-led news program to be used in the school's television system or over the school's intercom network.
24. Celebrate the different cultures and traditions that students bring to the school.
25. Begin a school character education newspaper (maybe title it *Character Conversations* or *Character Connections*).
26. Support student-led activities and make use of the student council and student clubs.
27. Show films and videos that examine the values in human behavior.

28. Launch projects that highlight a "value-a-month," such as "The Golden Rule."
29. Have banners and displays at the school entrance that show the values of the school.
30. Create a parent newsletter that helps them reinforce the values being taught at school.
31. Have students write stories, songs, and poems about values.
32. Create activities that promote a peaceful playground and conflict-resolution methods.
33. Have a special reading time where everyone is reading books or articles about values such as honesty or courage.
34. Monitor student behavior with regard to teasing and bullying and, if necessary, plan programs to lessen these behaviors, such as peer mediation.
35. Have each class take the responsibility for preparing a skit or story for a school assembly on a core value.
36. Have students suggest ways to improve conditions in the restrooms, cafeteria, parking lots, and playground.
37. Have students create placemats for the cafeteria that feature a value under study or how to behave when eating.
38. Have sessions for parents to help them know what the character education program is about and invite them to get involved.
39. Have the students write a pledge for all students, affirming the school's core values.
40. Ask teachers to share their activities that promote the core "value-a-month" with other teachers and with parents.
41. Create a buddy program for all new students.
42. Create a school bus program that promotes respect and responsibility.
43. Have a group of teachers and students create a monthly calendar, with suggestions for showing and practicing the "value-a-month."
44. Provide students and teachers with conflict-resolution and peer-mediation training.
45. Create programs around such themes as "Best Friends," "Character Counts," "Gratitude Is the Attitude," "Let's Be Courteous," or "Caring Is Sharing."
46. Ask teachers to hold class meetings where students can share in rule-making, airing concerns, and planning things to study.

47. Use posters, videos, contests, role-playing, and other activities to promote each of the school's core values.
48. Create an advisory system in which each student is placed in a group of ten to fifteen other students and meets with a staff member and other adults for at least thirty minutes each week, maybe at lunchtime.
49. Have a "rights and responsibilities" agreement that students and parents sign.
50. Ask your local newspaper to print stories about the school's character-education program and about students and groups who put the core values into practice.

PRACTICES AND PROMISES

The results of effective school studies reveal certain practices that show promise with regard to student behaviors and positive school climate. Fitch (1995)[4] provides this summary for your review.

Practices	*Promises*
	Increases in:
• site-based management	• student attendance
• shared decision making	• teacher attendance
• principal leadership	• job satisfaction
• high parental involvement	• student-parent satisfaction
• high expectations for students	• better student behavior
• time on task	• better teacher performance
• orderly school climate	• higher student achievement
• clean physical facilities	• trust
• frequent evaluation of student achievement	*Decreases in:*
	• student misbehaviors
• evaluation feedback to stakeholders	• graffiti
• staff development linked to goals	• vandalism
	• violence
	• student failures
	• student dropouts

In addition to Fitch's list, the promising practices that are keys to a caring, civil, and positive school climate are these:

- A safe, orderly environment
- Goals and a mission that include high expectations for student achievement and behavior.
- Moral and ethical leadership by the principal and other adults at the school.
- A management style, by the principal, that promotes shared decision making.
- School-wide discipline practices that uphold the school's core values and that are fair and evenly applied.
- Staff stability and active participation in the character development of all students.
- An infusion of the core values in the curriculum and all programs at the school.
- Instruction that teaches the core values and promotes cooperative learning and critical thinking.
- An active, democratically selected student government.
- Special school-wide programs that celebrate students' academic achievements, prosocial behaviors, and special talents.
- Student activities programs (co-curricular) that balance competition with sportsmanship and individualism with teamwork.
- Staff development that is ongoing, focusing on the moral responsibilities of teaching and guiding students.
- Parent and community involvement, participation, and support.
- The development of collaborative and collegial relationships among the adults and students at the school.
- Continued daily efforts by everyone at school to create a sense of community.
- The creation of a civil environment that attends to the language used at school and the manners displayed by students and adults.
- A renewed emphasis on citizenship carried out by students in service at home, school, and community.
- Continued attention, particularly by the administration, to "connecting" all of the components of the character education framework presented at Tour Stop 1.[5]

We have already made comments about the value of school-site leadership and management. We hope you appreciate our suggestion that, as principal, you pay close attention to your school's climate by institutionalizing the practices previously listed.

We now want to expand the effective-practices suggestions and the fifty ideas with some questions for you to ponder as you examine the climate of your school (also see Tour Stop 9). The list is not exhaustive. Our intent is to provide enough questions for you to add your own as you go about this self-examination in your efforts to fulfill promises (mission, expectations, goals) to the school's stakeholders.

EVALUATING THE SCHOOL CLIMATE

Measuring school climate can help us understand what was and what is, so that we can move forward to what could be.

(Freiberg, 1998)[6]

Using the set of indicators and suggestions by Elizabeth S. Foster-Harrison (1997),[7] we offer the following questions as a means of evaluating your school's climate.

Physical

1. How would a visitor to your school describe the physical facilities?
2. Is the building bright, well lighted, clean, and neat?
3. Is the playground and outside area well maintained, clean, and pleasing to the eye?
4. Is the school, both inside and outside, free of graffiti?
5. Are the colors in the school warm and inviting, fostering a relaxed environment?
6. Is there space for teachers, students, and others to engage in meaningful academic activities?
7. Does the staff have access to the basic tools to do its job (phones, computers, supplies)?
8. Is special attention given to bathrooms and the cafeteria?
9. Is student work displayed throughout the school and in classrooms?
10. Is the physical plant inspected regularly for safety and accident prevention?

Academic

1. Is there excitement about teaching and learning?
2. Are there high expectations to perform by both teachers and students?

3. Do teachers have the resources they need to provide quality instruction?
4. Are there opportunities for staff development and the discussion and sharing of ideas, strategies, and evaluation methods?
5. Are classrooms orderly and free from disruptions?
6. Do teachers employ a variety of individual and group strategies to engage students with the content of the subject matter?
7. Are support services available to teachers and students?
8. Do students and their parents receive regular feedback about the students' achievement?
9. Are there places for groups of students and teachers to meet and plan?
10. Are efforts made to involve parents in all aspects of the academic program?

Organizational

1. Do the staff and students get involved in the development and implementation of school policies?
2. Are members of all school committees represented on the school-site council or management team?
3. Are teachers empowered to view themselves as leaders?
4. Do committees in the school have clearly defined responsibilities that are related to the school's mission and goals?
5. Have school policies that impede and enhance student success been examined?
6. Have community resources and partners been identified and invited to participate in school affairs?
7. Is there oversight and monitoring of student and staff committees, as well as of the school-site management team or council?
8. Is the school a learning organization where all personnel are provided opportunities for learning and training to improve their skills and abilities?
9. Do you, the principal, take an active and supportive role in keeping the school focused on its mission and goals?
10. Do personnel at the school value the need for evaluation and feedback about organizational matters?

Socio-Emotional

1. How would stakeholders characterize the "feeling" of the school?
2. Is the climate such that adults like working there and students like learning there?

3. Is there a sense of trust, respect, and collegiality among teachers and staff?
4. Is the school a safe place to be?
5. Is there open, honest, and interactive communication?
6. Are there programs for students that address their social and emotional needs?
7. Do students have opportunities to interact with adults on a regular and sustained basis?
8. Do adults and student leaders address the concerns and issues of peer subcultures at the school?
9. Are programs offered to parents that address their child's social-emotional needs?
10. Are social-emotional programs integrated into the curriculum and the co-curricular activities?

The distinguishing feature of today's youth is not technology, it is aloneness . . . They are missing a coherent sense of community.

(Tell, 2000)[8]

CONCLUDING CLIMATE

At this stage in your tour, you have had the opportunity to read our views and ideas about planning character education initiatives for your school. We discussed the leadership responsibilities that you will have to assume and the importance of the school's climate as the incubator for helping students learn the core values of the program and the social-emotional behaviors that make for a caring, civil, and challenging educational experience.

Some principals may be evaluated, in part, on their performance in creating a positive school climate. For example, the Chula Vista Elementary School District (CA) plans to assess the principal's performance on several standards. One of the subcategories of Standard 3, The Principal Is Accountable for Customer Satisfaction, is the school culture. The performance descriptions are these:

Emerging: The principal is responsible for and collaborates with staff in establishing a culture that fosters mutual respect, fairness, pride, collegiality, trust, and excellence within the school community. The principal fosters a welcoming and inclusionary atmosphere. The principal makes positive connections with students, as demonstrated by their interactions with him/her.

Applying: The principal takes responsibility for creating a student leadership team, representative of all, that develops an ongoing process to address students rights, to hear student voices, and to ensure student-based decision making. The principal fosters a welcoming and inclusionary atmosphere for all staff, students, parents, and community.

Innovating: The entire school community demonstrates willingness to continuously examine its assumptions, beliefs, and practices in doing the work required for high levels of personal and organizational performances. The school culture reflects a customer-driven environment. There is an established process for addressing problems and mediating conflict.[9]

A nurturing, caring school environment is essential for instruction and for character development. At the next tour stop, we discuss the fifth component of the framework, which is teaching.

AN ELEMENTARY MODEL: LOKER SCHOOL, WAYLAND, MA

It is Monday morning and Principal Mary Sterling invites us into the school's cafeteria-gym to watch one of the school's weekly meetings.[10] We are ushered to our seats by fifth graders. We are joined by students, staff, and some parents. The meeting begins with a pledge to the flag, some songs, recognition of students' birthdays, announcements, and then presentations and performances by the students. The meeting lasts twenty-five minutes and we stay to talk to Principal Sterling. She tells us that school meetings are common in Britain and Japan. She says that the program varies each week and that there is much behind-the-scene preparation. In fact, she has students who will make presentation auditions in her presence. By auditioning, she tell us, students will know, with feedback, if they are ready for a public presentation. She and the teachers then work with the students, if necessary, to get them prepared for their performances. Another learning feature of the program, she points out, is that all students learn what it takes to be a member of an audience. Principal Sterling concludes by reminding our tour group that the "school meeting is a mirror of our school community because it reflects who we are and who we hope to be."[11]

A SECONDARY MODEL: OREM HIGH SCHOOL, UTAH

The tour group is met in the school parking lot by Professor J. Merrell Hansen and Principal John Childs.[12] They welcome us to this 1,600 student, grades 10–12 high school. The group members are impressed by the beautiful aquarium as they enter the school. Before talking about the school and its program, the group is taken on a tour. The chatter among members of the tour group reflects how impressed they are with the courtyards and foyers where students can gather to relax and enjoy the school. They comment on the use of the school's colors on the walls, the quotes from faculty that are posted on the walls, as well as the space made available for recognition of student achievement and for posting special events. They admire the student artwork that adorns the school cafeteria, the photographs in the foyers, and the artistic work by welding students that is displayed in the library courtyard. Two memorable areas are the "Skybrary," an open, window-lit facility, and Principal Childs's office, a "neat place" adorned by baseball caps, witty sayings, an antique post office box, an old soft drink machine, and a set of golf clubs.

In a comfortable meeting room the professor and principal talk about the school's programs, policies, and procedures. They discuss the rigorous academic curriculum; the unique interdisciplinary program called "Unified Studies" that includes social studies, science, language arts, and recreation. They describe their advanced placement courses, community service projects, and special programs such as ski trips; bird watching; "We the People," which is a national competition on the Constitution; a school-based reading program called "Project Literacy;" a "4.0 Party" for students with exceptional academic records; a ballroom dance club; and a jazz ensemble.

In response to questions about policies and processes, Principal Childs tells the group that the school "consciously tries to establish policies that

School Climate 61

encourage and permit rather than restrict or direct . . . [and] that seek a win/win result.[13] "He describes how they try to encourage all to participate, cooperate, and collaborate in the decision making by fostering a sense of belonging, openness, and trust.

Professor Hansen told the group that Orem High School was a member of John Goodlad's National Network for Education Renewal, which enables the administrators and faculty to share resources, expertise, and experiences with others in the network. He described the partnership program with Brigham Young University, especially the "cohort and associates" programs.

They conclude the orientation talk by telling our tour members: "We know, or are capable of knowing, how to create schools that have a positive and attractive climate. The challenge is to continually and consciously labor to achieve the goal—to make schools places where people like to be."[14]

E. F. DeRoche and M. M. Williams, *Educating Hearts and Minds: A Comprehensive Character Education Framework,* 2d ed. (Thousand Oaks, CA: Corwin Press, 2001).

J. Freiberg, *School Climate: Measuring, Improving, and Sustaining Healthy Learning Environments* (in press).

S. Johnson, "Does Your School's 'Family Culture' Expect Excellence?" *The High School Magazine* 5, no. 1 (1997): 26–29.

M. Marshall, *Fostering Social Responsibility* (Bloomington, IN: Phi Delta Kappa Fastback, no. 428, 1998).

H. Urban, *Life's Greatest Lessons or 20 Things I Want My Kids to Know* (Redwood City, CA: Great Lessons Press, 1997).

G. Vessels, *Character and Community Development: A School Planning and Teacher Training Handbook* (Westport, CT: Praeger, 1998).

Center for the Prevention of School Violence, *http://www.ncsu.edu/cpsv*.
Collaboration to Advance Social and Emotional Learning (CASEL), CASEL's Response to the Columbine Tragedy, *http://www.casel.org*.
The Tools for Change, *http://reviewing.co.uk/*.

REFERENCES

1. F. Lunenburg and A. Ornstein, *Educational Administration* (Belmont, CA: Wadsworth, 2000).

2. T. Deal and K. Peterson, *"Shaping School Culture: The Heart of Leadership"* (San Francisco, CA: Jossey Bass, 1999), 87–99.

3. K. Peterson and T. Deal, "How Leaders Influence the Culture of Schools." *Educational Leadership* 56, no. 1 (1998): 29.

4. C. Fitch, "School Organization and Class Scheduling: Conventional and Reformed." In J. Kaiser, ed., *The 21st Century Principal* (Mequon, WI: Stylex Publishing, 1995), 111, 115.

5. This list is gleaned from the recommendations of: T. Lickona, *Education for Character: How Our Schools Can Teach Respect and Responsibility* (New York, NY: Bantam Books, 1991), chap. 17.

6. H. J. Freiberg, "Measuring School Climate: Let Me Count the Ways." *Educational Leadership* 56, no. 1 (1998): 26.

7. E. Foster-Harrison, "Professional Climate: How Does Your School Compare?" *Schools in the Middle* 6, no. 5: 4–8.

8. C. Tell, "Generation What? Connecting with Today's Youth." *Educational Leadership* 57, no. 4 (2000): 12.

9. Chula Vista Elementary School District, *Principal Standards: Working Document* (Author, 2000).

10. M. Sterling, "Building a Community Week by Week." *Educational Leadership* 56, no. 1 (1998): 65–68.

11. M. Sterling, "Building a Community Week by Week." *Educational Leadership* 56, no. 1 (1998): 68.

12. J. M. Hansen and J. Childs, "Creating a School Where People Like to Be." *Educational Leadership* 56, no. 1 (1998): 14–17.

13. J. M. Hansen and J. Childs, "Creating a School Where People Like to Be." *Educational Leadership* 56, no. 1 (1998): 16.

14. J. M. Hansen and J. Childs, "Creating a School Where People Like to Be." *Educational Leadership* 56, no. 1 (1998): 17.

• *Tour Stop 5* •

Teaching

Effective teachers see the vital, inseparable relationship between the intellectual, physical, emotional, social, and moral growth of students.

—(E. L. Boyer, *The Basic School: A Community for Learning*, 1995)

Teaching is a moral activity and therefore needs special attention by you and the school's Character Education Council (CEC).

Teaching is a moral activity because it engages people in relationships.

Teaching is a moral activity because the purpose of teaching, of schooling in general, is to change student behaviors—what they learn, what they know, and how they act.

Teaching is a moral activity because teachers and other school personnel make judgments about what should be studied, how students should behave, and how they should spend their time.

Teaching is a moral activity because teaching is "a way of trying to make people better than they are, which means that it is always legitimate to ask questions about how well or how poorly the teacher's students are being treated. It is also legitimate to raise questions about how one person treats another, no matter what the relationship is to enter the domain of moral judgment."[1]

Teaching is a moral activity because: "What teachers say to children does matter, and because of this, classroom discourse is moral."

(Sockett, 1993)[2]

No matter how comprehensive a school's character education initiatives may look on paper, if the teachers do not have the attitude, interest, knowledge, and skill to implement these initiatives, then it is just another document taking up shelf space. So, the key question for this tour stop is: What do you and the CEC need to know about teaching for character development that can and should be shared with teachers in your school? We base our recommendations on information from the research on child development theories. Specifically, we describe how teachers create a classroom climate for learning and how teacher attitudes shape student learning. We provide you with details regarding the types of instructional strategies found to be very successful (the seven Cs). The seven Cs also provide hints about teacher preparation, roles, responsibilities, and classroom climate. We begin with two teaching models.

VIRTUES MODEL

The Center for the Advancement of Ethics and Character (CAEC) at Boston University created a teaching model "to help educators be more thoughtful and less haphazard in their efforts to educate for character." The CAEC suggests that their model, "internalizing virtue-knowing, loving, and doing the good," can be used through the curriculum, classroom management, and school-wide activities. Here is an explanation of each of the five principles in their model:

1. *Awareness* involves explaining and defining virtues as a means of building a common language and shared character goals for the school community. Students become aware that respect, kindness, and diligence matter when we talk about these words and remind them of their importance.
2. *Understanding* involves knowing what a virtue looks like and feels like lived. Understanding is enlightened through stories, poetry, images, and examples of lives past and present. Understanding helps us to love the good.
3. *Action* is about building good habits. We learn by doing. . . . It is about doing the good.
4. *Reflection* involves thinking about what we have done (a thoughtful examination of actions). . . . It is about knowing the good.
5. *Virtue* is the disposition to choose and act well. Virtue is at the heart of good character; it is the result of knowing, loving, and doing the good.[3]

VALUES MODEL

We find that teachers are overwhelmed by the many things they have to do in the classroom, with the content and standards of the subject matter that they teach, and with the pressure to raise test scores. To suggest to them that character education content needs to be given equal attention adds to their frustration. While many know that values should be infused into their curriculum and embedded in their classroom-management practices, they still ask for help.

So, after consultation with several teachers in our courses, academies, and workshops, we designed a teaching model that is particularly effective for teaching a specific value. The model focuses on four aspects of learning—awareness, analysis, application, and assessment (the four As). Awareness and analysis are paired, as are application and assessment. The paired aspects in the model are closely related and may become one in the teaching act. Although treated here separately for purposes of explanation, when the model is implemented, the teacher will note the relationship between the first two As of the model and the third and fourth As. The model is designed to help teachers structure their efforts to teach values. Its ultimate goal is to help students internalize values.

1. *Awareness:* The task for the teacher related to this aspect of the model is to introduce values to the students by helping them see the word that represents each value in a variety of settings throughout the school and in every classroom. It encourages them to use the word, define it, and practice using it in their speaking and writing exercises. They are encouraged to see how each value is used in the writing of others. The teacher explains the value and discusses it with his or her students. In this way, the teacher introduces the students to the language of values. Words reflect one's and society's attention to and appreciation of civility. Words reflect how you feel. Words, depending on how you use them, sometimes say a lot about who you are. Students, with guidance from the teacher, read, write, observe, and talk about each value—its meaning, its use, its purpose.
2. *Analysis:* In this aspect of the model, students study how each value (or vice, its opposite) is used in a variety of contexts, including newspapers, magazines, books, biographies, poetry, film, videos, the Internet, and in observing people's behaviors. The students reflect on how each value is operationalized by real-life

and fictional characters—how human beings demonstrate the value or vice. The keys to the analysis factor are questioning, critical thinking, and careful observation. Analysis, and the methods that foster it, should contribute to students' knowledge about the value; it should help students see why some people are able to demonstrate the value and others cannot or do not. It should help students appreciate how people live by the value, how people learn from their mistakes, and how people pay for their mistakes. Analysis activities assist students in internalizing each value—seeing how it leads to choices and consequences, how it is related to other values, and how it fosters or destroys relationships.

3. *Application:* This aspect of the model is about helping students apply each value in their daily lives. It is about practicing values in different settings and varying relationships. It is about practicing values so they become habits. Application means noting, from real life and literature, how people act on values. It is about observing how others practice, demonstrate, and foster values. Application means knowing what to do, why to do it, and how to do it. Application is about learning what happens when the value is used and what happens when it is not.

4. *Assessment:* The assessment aspect of the model means that the teacher and students examine the extent to which each value is applied in and out of the classroom. They verify the impact on relationships and behaviors. Through listening, questioning, observing, and practicing, they determine what worked and what did not and why. They decide what needs to be changed and what needs to be maintained. The assessment process is designed to raise the awareness level about each value under study. Its intent is to provide feedback to the teacher and students about how values have influenced the climate of the classroom, the interactions among students, and the extent to which values have an impact on achievement and behavior. Assessing requires students to apply the critical-thinking skills learned in the analysis aspect of the model to each of the three other aspects in the model. The assessment factor must address outcomes. It should help answer the question, What, if anything, has changed in our knowledge and behavior as a result of studying and practicing values?

AN EXAMPLE OF A MODEL

Terrence Quinn,[4] an elementary school principal, describes a useful model of how teachers in elementary schools can weave the core values of the character education program into the school day. Quinn explains how each school day begins with students using the school's public address system to make announcements (birthdays, events, etc.), read stories, recite poems, and quote "sayings" that relate to the monthly value as part of the "value-of-the-month program" (VAMP).

Quinn describes how teachers weave the values of "kindness and caring" into their curriculum. The value of "respect" is addressed in the study of animals; by studying water, students also learn "responsibility" for conservation and use of limited resources.

In language arts and social studies, the author talks about how teachers use real-life stories and historical figures that illustrate the application of values. For example, he says that students read about Cal Ripken (responsibility), Abraham Lincoln (honesty), Harriet Tubman (courage), Franklin Roosevelt and Bob Dole (perseverance), and *The Little Engine That Could* (persistence).

Teachers are encouraged to weave the values into lessons and relationships with students, in the everyday routines of the classroom and in their class rules, such as being punctual and prepared for class. Students are taught to be courteous to one another and to appreciate their classmates' contributions and performances at school assemblies.

Quinn talks about the "Kids Care Club," a community-service learning project that focuses on sick children, the poor, the elderly, and the handicapped.

As Quinn says, "Today, more than ever, education represents a moral as well as intellectual investment in our youth. . . . (I)t costs little or nothing to infuse core values into every aspect of school life."[5]

AN EXAMPLE OF A TEACHER ASSESSMENT: TEACHER'S VALUE MAP

In this example, teachers are asked to "map" teaching behaviors and strategies that contribute to or detract from fostering the values and behaviors that underscore the character education program. The positive methods can contribute to a "bank" of strategies that promote students' prosocial behaviors.

Directions: Please complete this survey and return it to the school secretary or to a member of the Character Education Evaluation Team (CEET). We will share the findings with you and discuss them at an in-service meeting.

1. List three to five things you and/or other teachers are doing to foster positive values, character, and prosocial behaviors in students.
2. Tell us two things you and/or other teachers should stop doing because you feel they detract from the character education program.
3. What should you and other teachers start doing?
4. Please complete these sentences:
    a. Our school is a place where _____.
    b. Students are rewarded in this school for _____.
    c. Teachers are rewarded in this school for _____.
    d. Relationships between teachers and students in this school _____.
    e. Relationships between teachers and parents in this school _____.
    f. The school's administration is _____.
    g. This school's character education program _____.
    h. For the most part, students in this school _____.
    i. The one wish I have for this school is _____.

TEACHER ATTRIBUTES

Let us add to what you already know about teachers and teaching. Although teaching styles vary enormously, your instructional leadership is evident when you help teachers successfully motivate students to become critical thinkers and responsible for their own learning. We start with Ernest Boyer's[6] observations about the four essential characteristics of effective teachers. He found that good teachers

1. are well informed (have broad knowledge and content-specific expertise);
2. know children (are attentive to the whole child);
3. empower students (use a variety of methods to encourage students to explore their own questions); and
4. are open, authentic human beings (maintain honest relationships with students).

 *A class in a school is a moral community where virtues should be studied and modeled and vices studied and opposed. There is a moral vocabulary, and there are moral concepts.*

(Etzioni, 1999)[7]

From the students' perspective, Bosworth[8] lists their perceptions of the characteristics of teachers who are caring educators. In our opinion, teachers in their role as character educators should attend to these behaviors. The students list the following attributes:

- ☐ helping with homework
- ☐ explaining work
- ☐ checking for understanding
- ☐ showing respect
- ☐ being tolerant
- ☐ valuing individuality
- ☐ being encouraging
- ☐ planning fun activities
- ☐ helping with personal problems
- ☐ providing guidance (providing direction, goal-setting activities, and advice)
- ☐ going the extra mile: teachers extend themselves beyond the job (e.g., staying after school to help students with their work—talking to students about their problems)
- ☐ being nice, polite
- ☐ wanting to help students
- ☐ being success-oriented (believing in students' capabilities)
- ☐ being involved (friendly, modeling, trusting, truthful)

This checklist provides an excellent overview of essential characteristics, but for character education to be effective, we need to further describe the specific details about what teachers do when they demonstrate these qualities.

We discovered that teachers who teach for student cognitive and character development model the characteristics and skills that support the literature on effective teaching. All of the parameters of teaching (knowledge; ability to manage classroom environments, apply curriculum standards, use a variety of strategies, and assess student outcomes) are interrelated—what a teacher does in one area affects the others.

 *Values aren't inherited, they are learned . . . Parents, schools, and communities provide the experiences and education that help shape a child's choices.*

(Bohlin, 2000)[9]

Teachers make the difference. A number of researchers[10] have determined that certain teacher characteristics or attributes enable them to be more successful in having a long-term, positive impact on student behaviors. According to Leming, "teachers inevitably play a crucial role in constructing the parameters of the complex social settings where character education takes place."[11] What the research shows is that regardless of the quality of the program in use, teacher characteristics and attributes have a significant influence on student outcomes. These findings provide, in our opinion, lists of behaviors that teachers can attend to in their role as character educators.

Leming[12] sums up the characteristics of the effective character educator as being competent (teaching well), a model of good character (trustworthy, honest), and caring (creates caring relationships). What students think matters. In many instances, what is most important is that the teacher is perceived by students to have a particular attribute. We now offer a framework of teacher attributes that matches up with research findings.[13]

TEACHING FRAMEWORK: THE SEVEN CS

In addition to incorporating informal activities and attending to teacher attributes, we have developed and field tested a set of teaching strategies that teachers can use to infuse character education practices and processes into just about any lesson. We built these teaching strategies into a framework we call the seven Cs: connections, constructivism, classroom management, critical thinking, conflict resolution, cooperative learning, and citizenship (see chart 5.2). We encourage teachers to use all of these strategies.

Teachers "do" character education best when they infuse it into the process and content of their lessons. Whichever strategy a teacher chooses, he or she should be prepared to adapt the strategy to match up with curricular goals and instructional objectives at the grade level appropriate for the students. These teaching strategies will facilitate student

☐ Connections
  *relationship connections
  *head-heart-hand connections
  *content connections
☐ Constructivism
  *student-centered
  *authentic
☐ Critical Thinking
  *Socratic questioning
  *student-generated questions
  *ethical decision making
☐ Classroom Management
  *classroom climate
  *class meetings
☐ Cooperative Learning
  *activities that require:
    task interdependence
    role interdependence
    reward interdependence
☐ Conflict Resolution
  *peer mediation
  *"I" messages
  *problem-solving strategies
☐ Citizenship
  *democratic practices
  *student-generated class rules
  *community service learning

Chart 5.2
Teaching Framework the Seven Cs

learning, which can be demonstrated on assessment measures. Character education teaching strategies do not work effectively if they are not linked to curricular goals (see Tour Stop 7) and assessments (see Tour Stop 9). Training related to these and other instructional strategies is the emphasis of the next tour stop.

Both you and the CEC should work with teachers to expand on and "deepen" their use of the seven Cs. Many of these strategies will be familiar to you and your teachers. Books and articles have been written on the importance of each one. Most, if not all, character education experts agree on the importance of the seven Cs. So, our plan here is simply to outline some of our thoughts about how each of the seven Cs applies to teaching for character.

STRATEGY ONE: CONNECTIONS

Teachers and students have to learn to make connections between what they say, feel, and do. That is, they need to focus on relationships and the "connectedness" of things. Kohn,[14] in 1999, describes the "fragmentation" of students' learning experiences. He says, "One kind of learning is separated from another... One subject is separated from another.... One task is separated from another.... Learning is separated from doing.... One student is separated from another."

The components of the framework in this book are connected. This teaching framework connects the strategies. To have the greatest influence on student academic learning and character development, the strategies should be implemented "wholly." That is, using only one or two of them may not be as effective as using all seven strategies. As you read our commentary about each component of this teaching framework, you will see the value of connectedness as it applies to teachers and their teaching. For example, a teacher's attention to the climate of the classroom will be enhanced when applying ideas for resolving conflict or using methods to create cooperative learning groups.

One more example of what we mean by "connectedness" is found in an article by Schaps.[15] He reports on a study in which 12,000 students in grades 7–12 were interviewed about their experiences in eight different "high-risk" areas—violence, suicidal tendencies, emotional distress, use of alcohol/marijuana/tobacco, sexual activity, and pregnancy. Researchers asked the students to identify factors that might help them resist these risks. Schaps says that only two factors were found to reduce involvement in these risky behaviors (except pregnancy); they were connected to family and connected to school. As Schaps says, "The more connected students felt to their families, the less involved they were in risky behavior...." The more connected they were to their school—"feeling close to people at school, feeling fairly treated by teachers, feeling part of one's school"—the less likely they were to engage in risky behaviors.

The importance of connectedness is highlighted by Tell,[16] who reminds us of the view of Patricia Hersch. In her book *The Tribe Apart,* she suggests that the distinguishing feature of today's youth is not technology but aloneness. Tell says, "Because of the social changes of the past twenty-five years, teens today have spent more time alone than any other generation. They are missing a coherent sense of community."

STRATEGY TWO: CONSTRUCTIVISM

Most educators are looking for a strong link to a theory or philosophy of education to match with character education initiatives. We find that "constructivism" fits best with the strategies, processes, and content of character education as presented in this book.

What is constructivism? It is based on the premise that we all construct our own perspective of the world, through individual experiences and schema. Constructivism, according to Schuman (1996),[17] focuses on preparing the learner to problem solve in ambiguous situations.

Following are some basic assumptions of constructivism that were outlined by Merrill in 1991.[18]

   a. Knowledge is constructed from experience.
   b. Learning is a personal interpretation of the world.
   c. Learning is an active process in which meaning is developed on the basis of experience.
   d. Conceptual growth comes from the negotiation of meaning, the sharing of multiple perspectives, and the changing of our internal representations through collaborative learning.
   e. Learning should be situated in realistic settings; testing should be integrated with the task and not a separate activity.

Effective methods are needed for organizing knowledge that will result in simplifying, generating new propositions, and increasing the manipulation of information. In this way, students will construct their own understanding of what they learn. A synthesis of Bruner's[19] theory of instruction addresses four major aspects of constructivism that coincide with character education:

1. Instruction must be concerned with the experiences and contexts that make the student willing and able to learn (readiness).
2. Instruction must be structured so that the student can easily grasp it (spiral organization).
3. Instruction should be designed to facilitate extrapolation and/or fill in the gaps (going beyond the information given).

4. The nature and pacing of rewards and punishments motivate students to learn.

Knowing that theories are just one part of the picture, it is crucially important to help teachers connect what they are learning about constructivism to their classroom teaching practices. Brooks and Brooks[20] have the most well-developed set of instructional strategies for constructivism. We have taken their generic teaching strategies and adapted them for "character education." The following twelve strategies suggest ways for teachers to be constructivist character educators:

1. Character educators encourage and accept student autonomy and initiative.
2. Character educators use raw data and primary sources, along with manipulative, interactive, and physical materials.
3. When framing tasks, character educators use cognitive terminology such as "classify," "analyze," "predict," and "create."
4. Character educators allow student responses to drive lessons, shift instructional strategies, and alter content as necessary to be responsive to students' needs.
5. Character educators inquire about students' understanding of concepts before sharing their own understandings of those concepts.
6. Character educators encourage students to engage in dialogue, both with the teacher and with one another.
7. Character educators encourage student inquiry by asking good questions and encouraging students to ask questions of each other.
8. Character educators seek elaboration of students' responses and thereby create a sense of mutual trust and respect in the classroom.
9. Character educators engage students in experiences that create cognitive dissonance and then encourage discussion.
10. Character educators allow wait time after posing questions.
11. Character educators provide time for students to construct relationships, create metaphors, and apply ideas.
12. Character educators nurture students' natural curiosity through frequent use of the learning-cycle model. (The learning-cycle model consists of discovery, concept introduction, and concept application, which is similar to the four As discussed earlier.)

Teachers need to develop these skills fully to become constructivist character educators (see Tour Stop 6 for training and staff development ideas).

STRATEGY THREE: CRITICAL THINKING

Students must be educated to feel what wise people know: the more you learn, the more you are aware of your ignorance. Since it is impossible to teach everything we know to be of value, we must equip students with the ability to keep questioning.

(Wiggins, 1996)[21]

Critical thinking is an essential process in making a judgment or evaluating personal experiences and the experiences of others. A requirement for thinking critically includes the skill of question asking. Teaching for character is helping students learn to think critically. It seems that many students follow instructions, perform tasks, or get themselves into situations without the skills of thinking about what they are doing and why they are doing it. Helping students to "talk to themselves" (metacognition), to listen to their inner voice (conscience), to ask questions and think through problems (reasoning), and to find alternatives and seek solutions are the essentials of critical thinking for character development.

Critical thinking is "connected" to cooperative learning, classroom climate, constructivism, and citizenship. Critical thinking is an essential part of character education because it helps students learn to compare their experiences with others and to clarify and refine their ideas, perceptions, notions, problems, and behaviors. Critical thinking offers students ways to explore problems, question actions and behaviors, and examine alternative possibilities, choices, and solutions. Critical thinking offers teachers the opportunity to use fiction (stories, myths, fables, parables) and nonfiction (biographies, media stories, heroes and heroines, real-life dilemmas) as the content for moral lessons by helping students use a "values lens" to question and discuss what they see, read, hear, and do.

Three essential aspects of critical thinking that we use in our character education courses and professional-development seminars are question asking, the "Socratic method," and "Bloom's Taxonomy." A few comments about these "critical thinking" strategies may be helpful.

Elkind and Sweet[22] state the best case for using the Socratic method. "This is a powerful teaching method because it actively engages the learner and forces critical thinking, which is just what is needed in examining ethics, values, and other character issues." They provide a sample lesson plan, offer some examples, suggest ways to facilitate using the method, and conclude that their experience using the Socratic method approach helps students "become ethical, respectful, responsible people who think critically, solve problems nonviolently, and make choices based on what's right instead of what they can get away with."[23]

In addition to the Socratic method, simulation, case studies, and specific classroom strategies help teachers improve their question-asking skills and model the use of critical-thinking skills. Following are a couple of examples.

To help students analyze a historical event, current event, or a conflict between two people, including themselves, teachers can use what we call "Give Me Five." The student is shown that each finger on his or her hand is one of the five "W" questions: What happened? When did it happen? Where did it happen? Who was involved? Why did it happen? The palm of the hand has the question: How did it happen? Teachers have also used "Give Me Five" successfully to help students reflect on conflict situations in the classroom or on the playground.

To help teachers keep in mind the taxonomy of thinking skills developed by Bloom when they are teaching or preparing assignments for students, we created a mnemonic we call "KCAASE" (K-see): knowledge, comprehension, application, analysis, synthesis, and evaluation.

We modified behavior strategies developed by others and encourage teachers to help students become STARS. We tell teachers that this is a problem-solving method to show students that they are responsible for their actions and to provide them with a tool for thinking through their behaviors. Some teachers cut out stars and give them to students at the beginning of the school year. On the "star" the student will read:

> STOP = Hold it! Stop it! Don't do it! Cool it!
> THINK = About what you are going to do! About the A-B-C (alternatives, better choices, consequences)!
> ACT = Is it best for you? Is it right? Is it your only choice? Do it!
> REFLECT = Was it your best choice? If yes, why? If not, why not?
> START = Second chance! Do it again! Do it differently!

One more example: If teachers are really going to encourage students to use critical-thinking skills, they should do the same. One example we use is to have teachers, particularly teachers in middle and high schools, reflect on the why and how of homework assignments they give students. Here is what our self-analysis handout looks like.

DO I

1. introduce the homework in class?
2. explain its purpose and importance?
3. set the conditions for its completion?
4. explain how it will be graded?
5. tell students how I can help them?
6. know what students should get out of it?

WOULD I

7. like to do this assignment?
8. take a chance and be more creative?
9. find this assignment motivating and interesting?

SHOULD I

10. survey students about my homework assignments?
11. consider their other responsibilities?
12. individualize assignments?
13. try new ideas?
14. let them create some of their own assignments?

Several major educational organizations, like ASCD, and many commercial publishers offer programs and curricular material on critical thinking.[24] The important point here is that you, your teachers, and others see the need to help students become critical thinkers. This important character-development skill will enable students to make wise decisions, to resist peer pressure, to better understand the messages from the media, and to increase the probability that each will behave ethically.

STRATEGY FOUR: CLASSROOM CLIMATE

Everybody has ability, but pride in performance is what makes the difference.

Vince Lombardi

Much has been written about classroom climate. So, what caveats of advice can we bring to you at this "vista point" in our character education tour? At Tour Stop 4, we talked about the importance of a positive, caring, and civil school climate. A school that develops a caring community, with classrooms that capture this sense of community in its relationship between teachers and students, and students and students, will have a positive impact on student behavior, work habits, and achievement.[25]

In a nutshell, a classroom fostering the school's sense of community and its core values will be one that is caring, civil (moral/ethical practices), and democratic (responsible self-governance); that has high expectations for both academics and behavior, where values are practiced and vices opposed, and where each of the seven Cs described at this tour stop are implemented.

Our focus here is on a strategy for creating a positive classroom climate—class meetings. As DeVries and Zan[26] point out, class meetings help children engage in self-governance, think about specific social and moral issues (note the connection to critical thinking), and thus build an active community of learners. Here are seven reasons why teachers should hold class meetings:

1. students share ownership of the classroom;
2. improves students' moral reasoning;
3. enhances listening and speaking skills;
4. creates a place where students' thoughts and ideas are valued;
5. provides an arena to focus on the school's core values;
6. establishes a structure for conducting class business; and
7. provides opportunities for teachers to teach and for students to learn the skills of participation, cooperation, problem solving, and democratic decision making.

Let us share with you a teacher's view in the following composite of our discussions with teachers on this topic.

> I use class meetings at least once a day, sometimes twice, for about twenty to thirty minutes. I find these meetings to be a way for me to connect with my students and for them to connect with one another. In these meetings, we share our concerns, problems, issues, and ideas. We discuss solutions to problems and consider suggestions for making

the classroom a better place to teach and learn. We practice active listening and speaking civilly.

We talk about the value of the month and discuss how best to practice it. We create classroom rules and identify the consequences for not following them. We also use this time to conduct the business of the class. Sometimes we just engage in informal conversation about things that have happened to the students in and out of school. Sometimes we talk about what we have read in newspapers or seen on television, particular news about how people behave and why we think they do what they do.

In the morning, I usually have them practice greeting each other, talk about manners, ask them to share their goals for the day, and go over our class objectives. We review classroom assignments and responsibilities for the day. I review my lesson plans for them and we talk about motivation, attention, and time schedules.

If I have a class meeting at the end of the school day we discuss what the students learned; how they applied the values they are studying, if in fact they did; who feels they had a good and/or bad day and why; and what they have to do for homework and who will need help doing it. Then, I give them a few minutes to reflect in their "value journals" on their actions and behaviors during the day.

I regularly use questions to get them thinking about things. I also use questionnaires (survey on differing topics) to get their views on things because not all of my students like to share their thoughts in front of the whole class. Then, I summarize the information, prepare a short report, and engage them in a discussion of the findings. The more I find out about them and they about each other, the closer we come together as a "family." That's the metaphor I use on a daily basis—this class is our family and we will experience the joys, problems, and tasks that are found in most families.

Class meetings, to make an important point once again, are but one of several effective strategies for developing students' character and fostering the core values of the school. The strategies presented in this and at other tour stops must be "connected." They can be independent; that is, teachers can hold class meetings, but for meetings to be an effective component of the school's character education initiatives, they must be supported by a positive school climate, by cooperative learning opportunities, by a sense of service, and by a value-rich curriculum and co-curricular programs.

STRATEGY FIVE: COOPERATIVE LEARNING

Cooperative learning arrangements promote . . . prosocial interaction among students who differ in achievement, gender, race, or ethnicity . . . Cooperative methods also . . . have positive effects . . . on affective outcomes such as self-esteem, academic self-confidence, liking and feeling liked by classmates, and various measures of empathy and social cooperation.

(Good and Brophy, 2000)[27]

We all know a lot about cooperative learning. However, cooperative learning is one of the most misunderstood methodologies we have seen implemented. What we observe for the most part is *group work,* not *cooperative learning.* What teachers call cooperative learning consists of groups of students completing a worksheet or set of questions together in class. To be true cooperative learning, three elements must be present; they are task interdependence, role interdependence, and reward interdependence. When these three elements are present, cooperative learning is one of the single best strategies for helping students reach character education objectives and for having positive effects on student achievement.

According to the original research by Johnson and Johnson[28] conducted on the effects of cooperative learning on student behavior, we note several student outcomes as a result of participating in cooperative-learning activities that also match up with objectives for character education programs. We present them to you as a checklist that teachers can use for assessing student outcomes after they have participated in cooperative-learning activities over a period of time.

Student Outcomes Checklist

- ☐ Student achievement is higher.
- ☐ Greater competencies exist in:
  Critical thinking,
  Attitude toward subjects, and
  Working collaboratively.
- ☐ Students perceive grading as "fair."
- ☐ Students maintain positive relationships:
  Acceptance of diverse students and
  Higher levels of self-esteem.
- ☐ Students manifest greater cognitive and affective perspective-taking (vs. egocentrism).

We highly recommend having teachers go through additional training in cooperative-learning strategies in order to implement the method in such a way as to ensure that student outcomes, like the ones listed previously, are reached. The only time we have seen success is when teachers actually participate in training activities containing all three elements (task, role, and reward interdependence). It is crucial that teachers do two things with students to guarantee success of the method: (1) provide time in class for direct training of students in the skills of social cooperation and (2) supervise students closely while giving them relevant feedback. Once teachers experience the power of cooperative learning, they can use this method to help students learn skills of social cooperation that will enable them to reach the student outcomes listed previously.

STRATEGY SIX: CONFLICT RESOLUTION

If we are to reach real peace in this world, and if we are to carry on a real war against war, we shall have to begin with the children.

Mahatma Gandhi

Conflict is a part of everyday life. Conflict is a natural part of relationships and results any time there is miscommunication of ideas or tension with ideology. Minor conflicts and disagreements can turn into major problems unless we have the skills and dispositions to deal with the conflict early on. Many of us are uncomfortable with conflict and lack the skills/knowledge necessary to deal with conflict constructively.

With ever-increasing levels and types of violence occurring in schools and classrooms, and with teacher concerns about school safety, violence, and disruptive student behaviors, the need for teachers and students to develop knowledge and skills relating to problem solving, conflict resolution, and dispute mediation is obvious. Discipline policies that regulate student behavior should also include ways to help students understand how to solve problems and resolve conflicts peacefully.

Conflict Resolution: One Simple Method

Most schools apply a conflict-resolution program school-wide. There is one very simple method of solving problems, which has been the most helpful at resolving conflicts in classrooms. Gordon's[29] No-Lose problem-solving method includes the following six steps:

Step 1: Define the problem.
Step 2: Brainstorm solutions.
Step 3: Evaluate solutions.
Step 4: Decide on the solution to try.
Step 5: Determine how to implement the decision.
Step 6: Evaluate the final solution.

Problem-solving methods like Gordon's help students learn how to resolve conflicts peacefully. When we reviewed the research, we found similar student outcomes for conflict resolution as we found for cooperative learning. We strongly encourage you to provide workshops and training for teachers related to these two methods. Combined, they can have a powerful influence on student behaviors.

STRATEGY SEVEN: CITIZENSHIP

Our aim should be to make people more responsible. What we ought to be asking is not "what should you be entitled to?" but "what should you be responsible for?" . . . To restore citizenship is the central requirement of a post-capitalist polity.

(Drucker, 1993)[30]

It seems that in our society today, voter turnout is the lowest it has ever been. Cynicism about government and those who run it reigns. Apathy is apparent. Young people are largely indifferent to civic matters. Positive role models are missing. Demanding one's rights has far outstripped the sense of responsibility. *Pluribus* is plentiful, *unum* scarce.

Citizenship is not a spectator sport; nor is it "bowling alone"; nor is it being a "tribe apart." Citizenship is knowing and doing. It involves education and participation. Given this state of affairs, the need for character education coupled with civic education is apparent. In light of these concerns, then, we pose four questions for you and the CEC:

1. What does it mean to be a citizen in your school? In your community?
2. What has to be done in your school to revive civic education and couple it with your character education efforts?

3. What does the citizenship side of the students' report cards really mean to the teachers, students, and parents in your school?
4. What is the relationship between character education and civic education?

The answer to the last question is provided by the Center for Civic Education.[31] The center's view is that while the two are not synonymous, they are connected. "Fostering public character and certain aspects of private character are essential elements of civic education. Good public character can hardly exist in the absence of good private character traits such as honesty and civility. The aims of civic and character education, therefore, overlap in important respects."

The aims of both programs are shaped by the school culture. Schaps and Lewis[32] tell us that "schools inescapably influence children's civic development through the content they teach directly... (and) through the hidden curriculum of relationships with others, classroom management and discipline, and organizational climate and policies." Salomone (2000)[33] reminds us that "the school itself must exist as a morally coherent community and as a microcosm of democracy, creating a cohesive institutional ethos that persistently reinforces notions of democratic rights and responsibilities at all levels."

Both character and civic education can bring focus and meaning to the citizenship side of report cards. Character-building citizenship programs in your school will not only encourage the internalization of the core values but will couple these with the democratic values of justice, fairness, courage, empathy, and the like. The melding of the two programs should help students develop an *awareness* of the purposes and meaning of citizenship in a democratic society. It should add to an *appreciation* of life in a democratic society. It should lead to an *analysis* of what works and what needs attention about government, group, and individual behaviors. Finally, both programs must include *action,* which is the belief that one person or one group can do things that serve the common good, the belief that participation matters.

Thus, we start early. Teachers start by helping children begin to develop the habits of citizenship and good character on the first day a child enters school. Then, we expand the opportunities. Teachers not only provide students with the opportunity to learn civics but they take them beyond the four walls of the classroom and get them to witness democracy in action.

We solve civic problems. Teachers guide students in completing community projects and engaging in service learning.

We bear witness. Teachers use media, provide field trips, or invite guest speakers to provide students with the opportunity to witness government at work.

We model. Teachers create classrooms that are democratically oriented. Principals push for a school culture of caring, civility, empathy, and commitment.

We connect. Teachers connect civics with character, civics with critical thinking, civics with cooperative learning, civics with classroom climate, and civics with conflict resolution.

TOUR THOUGHTS

At this tour stop, we highlighted something you already know—"It's what's up front that counts!" What happens in the classroom between the teacher and his or her students is really what matters, both academically and with character education. Thus, your role as the school principal and the CEC's role as the leader of the school's character education efforts necessitates that particular attention be paid to teachers and teaching. Teachers must model the core values. Teachers must use strategies that engage students in learning the values. Teachers must create classrooms that are democratically managed. Teachers must encourage and engage students in moral reasoning, ethical decision making, and moral action. Teachers must realize that through their words, strategies, materials, and relationships with students and other adults at the school, they have a powerful and long-lasting influence on students. Teachers must also appreciate the fact that they cannot be character educators in isolation from the community in which the school is located, from the parents and guardians of the students at the school, and from the community at-large. Teaching for character is and has to be a team effort; it does take a village.

At this tour stop, we shared our "best" strategies for teachers. This tour stop is directly linked with the next, where we present ways to develop, train, and assess teachers as character educators. The teacher-planning guide, self-assessment checklist, and teacher evaluation checklist presented at the next tour stop can be used by teachers and administrators as guides in staff development and training and also for assessing the effectiveness of integrating character education practices into lessons and activities.

PARTNERS FOR PEACE, LUCY V. BARNSLEY ELEMENTARY SCHOOL IN ROCKVILLE, MARYLAND

It's Monday, so it must be Maryland.[34] And it is. Our tour bus takes us to Lucy V. Barnsley Elementary School in Rockville, Maryland. This school might be called the "peace school." Greeting us as we step off the bus is Liz Sutherland, a teacher at the school. (Note: the following was written by Elizabeth Sutherland for this tour stop.)

Liz leads us into the school, where we are welcomed by the principal, Ms. Annan. As we tour the school, Liz tells us about the school and the peace program. Barnsley Elementary is home to approximately 650 students and is a microcosm of Montgomery County Public Schools. Barnsley is one of six elementary schools that feed into one middle and one high school. Ms. Annan is open to and supportive of the teachers who work for her. She encourages the staff to dream about how things can be and then gives them the opportunity to try things out.

In the summer of 1999, I approached Ms. Annan with an idea—"Partners for Peace." I, like everyone else, was deeply concerned and disturbed by the Columbine High School incident in Colorado. I had seen a local newscaster present a report about how students, staff, and the community were marching in a Peace Parade at an elementary school in Prince George's County in Maryland. They were celebrating 162 days of peace. I started to think about what we could do at Barnsley to promote peace. I thought that focusing on peace at a school at the beginning of the year might actually improve the time spent with students and decrease the time spent dealing with conflict. Calling the program "Partners for Peace," I recommended that we work on the initiative together, starting in each of the elementary schools in our cluster and continuing as the students moved through the school system. The cluster agreed to adopt it as our character education program.

A staff meeting was held to introduce "Partners for Peace" to the staff. I provided an outline of ideas and activities. Teachers asked their students what they could do in the classroom and throughout the school to make the year a peaceful one. Each class wrote a set of rules and/or a constitution in the form of a "Peace Pledge," which were presented at a school-wide assembly. T-shirts, with a "Partners for Peace" logo, were designed. When staff wore these at the Peace Pep Rally (assembly), it was extremely effective in showing staff unity in the effort to keep peace. The goal for all students and staff was to keep peace at Barnsley. Peace Pledges were shared and posted outside each classroom. Each classroom displayed a "Days of Peace" sign to help people keep track of the number of peace days achieved at Barnsley. Each morning student announcers gave peace quotations to start the day in a peaceful manner. Instructional assistants hung huge laminated signs in the cafeteria on how to make the lunchroom a "peaceful" place to eat. *All* staff members used peace vocabulary throughout the day to reinforce our efforts.

At the end of each month, students were given an opportunity to nominate a classmate as "Peace Keeper of the Month." Student nominations were to include specific examples of how the classmate kept peace or prevented peace from being broken. Peace Keepers were rewarded with Peace Keeper Certificates and Peace Paw Pins (school mascot is a cougar). Pictures of all the Peace Keepers were proudly posted on a bulletin board in the front hall.

Student council members decided that a Peace Committee was necessary to manage and motivate peace throughout the school. They decided to make the announcement at the end of each day about whether peace had been achieved or broken at Barnsley. Any time a conflict occurred and/or peace was broken, the students involved were required to fill out a peace report documenting the event. Peace reports were sent home and required a parent signature.

In order to keep motivation high, students were rewarded at the end of each twenty-day period with a peace party. Children brainstormed party ideas and each class voted on the ideas. In January, the Peace Committee decided to have a door-decorating activity. The theme was *Opening Doors to a Peaceful Millennium*. Peace skits were produced, written, and performed by students. At the end of the year, students on the Peace Committee decided to have a peace sale to raise money for a school project. They raised enough to plant a peace garden in the front of the school. Families and staff had an opportunity to purchase personally engraved "Peace Bricks" that were added to the garden.

Specialists at the school were very involved in the Partners for Peace initiative. The art teacher in our school had art lessons that included peace posters, flags, and a peace quilt (hung in the main hall). The music teacher integrated the theme of peace into the songs and music she taught students. Our school counselor taught lessons and strategies with a peace/conflict resolution theme. Parents in the community jumped on the peace wagon as well. A parent in the PTA in charge of organizing and scheduling cultural arts performances selected performers who focused on and included a peace theme. Students on the Peace Committees at each of the cluster schools were invited to share the peace initiatives taking place at their schools at the Rockville High School Community Health and Safety Fair.

Throughout the year, students, teachers, staff members, and the community embraced "peace." We finished the school year with 84 days of peace. Our goal for this coming school year is to beat 84 days and get as close to 180 days as possible. As with any new program you have to start somewhere. We decided we would count the number of peace days, use peace vocabulary, make peace pledges, and tie in the theme of peace wherever and whenever possible. The key is to truly believe in what you are doing and commit yourself to it. If the staff buys into it, the kids and parents will, too. According to the response from the staff, students, and community, Partners for Peace was a success. We will use this year as our benchmark and use data collected from the peace reports and attendance records as further documentation of the program's success. Good luck with whatever program you choose. PEACE!

After answering our questions, Liz bid us "bon voyage" as our tour bus headed west to our next tour stop.

S. S. Cohen, "The Moral Future of Our Children." *Parents* 75, no. 2 (2000): 86–92.
D. W. Johnson, R. T. Johnson, E. J. Holubec, and P. Roy, *Circles of Learning: Cooperation in the Classroom* (Alexandria, VA: Association for Supervision and Curriculum Development, 1984).
T. R. Sizer and N. F. Sizer, *The Students Are Watching: Schools and the Moral Contract* (Boston: Beacon Press, 1999).
L. Wiley, *Comprehensive Character-Building Classroom: A Handbook for Teachers* (DeBray, FL: Longwood Communications, 1998).
E. A. Wynne, "Character Development: Renewing an Old Commitment." *Principal* 65, no. 3 (1986): 28–31.

The Developmental Studies Center, http://www.devstu.org.
Institute for Global Ethics, http://www.globalethics.org.
Teaching Peace, http://www.teachingpeace.org.
The Yale Child Study Center—School Development Program, http://pandora.med.yale.edu/comer/welcome.html.

REFERENCES

1. P. Jackson, R. Boostrom, and D. Hansen, *The Moral Life of Schools* (San Francisco, CA: Jossey Bass, 1993), 173.

2. H. Sockett, *The Moral Base for Teacher Professionalism* (New York, NY: Teachers College Press, 1993), 14.

3. D. Farmer, "Internalizing Virtue: Putting the Model to Work." *Character* 7, no. 2 (1999): 4.

4. T. Quinn, "Weaving Values into the School Day." *Principal* 76, no. 3 (1997): 54–55.

5. T. Quinn, "Weaving Values into the School Day." *Principal* 76, no. 3 (1997): 55.

6. E. L. Boyer, *The Basic School: A Community for Learning* (Princeton, NJ: The Carnegie Foundation for the Advancement of Teaching, 1995), 41–43.

7. A. Etzioni, "The Truths We Must Face to Curb School Violence." *Education Week* 18, no. 39 (1999): 57.

8. K. Bosworth, "Caring for Others and Being Cared for." *Phi Delta Kappan* 26, no. 9 (1995): 686–693.

9. K. Bohlin, in S. S. Cohen, "The Moral Future of Our Children." *Parents* 75, no. 2 (2000): 86–92.

10. J. Leming, "Applied Ethics or Character Education?: Contrasting Approaches to the Development of Moral Teachers" (paper presented at the annual meeting of the American Association of Colleges of Teacher Education, Chicago, February 2000); M. Williams, "Actions Speak Louder Than Words: What Students Think about Character Education." *Educational Leadership* 51, no. 3 (November 1993); and T. Good and G. Brophy, *Looking in Classrooms,* 8th ed. (New York, NY: Longman, 2000).

11. J. Leming, "Applied Ethics or Character Education?: Contrasting Approaches to the Development of Moral Teachers" (paper presented at the annual meeting of the American Association of Colleges of Teacher Education, Chicago, February 2000), 1.

12. J. Leming, "Applied Ethics or Character Education?: Contrasting Approaches to the Development of Moral Teachers" (paper presented at the annual

meeting of the American Association of Colleges of Teacher Education, Chicago, February 2000).

13. M. Williams, "Actions Speak Louder Than Words: What Students Think about Character Education." *Educational Leadership* 51, no. 3 (November 1993).

14. A. Kohn, *The Schools Our Children Deserve* (Boston, MA: Houghton Mifflin, 1999), 67–70.

15. E. Schaps, "Community in School: A Key to Violence, Character Formation, and More." *Character Education* 8, no. 2 (2000): 1.

16. C. Tell, "Generation What? Connecting with Today's Youth." *Educational Leadership* 57, no. 4 (2000): 12.

17. L. Schuman, "Perspectives on Instruction," *http://edweb.sdu.edu/courses/edtec540/Perspectives/Perspectives.html*.

18. M. D. Merrill, "Constructivism and Instructional Design." *Educational Technology* (May 1991): 45–53.

19. J. Bruner, *Toward a Theory of Instruction* (Cambridge, MA: Harvard University Press, 1966).

20. J. G. Brooks and M. G. Brooks, *In Search of Understanding: The Case for Constructivist Classrooms* (Alexandria, VA: Association for the Supervision and Curriculum Development, 1993), chap. 9.

21. G. Wiggins, "The Futility of Trying to Teach Everything of Importance." *Educational Leadership* 47, no. 3 (1996): 48.

22. D. Elkind and F. Sweet, "The Socratic Approach to Character Education." *Educational Leadership* (May 1997): 56.

23. D. Elkind and F. Sweet, "The Socratic Approach to Character Education." *Educational Leadership* (May 1997): 59.

24. Association for Supervision and Curriculum Development, *www.ascd.org*.

25. E. Schaps, C. Lewis, and M. Watson, "Building Community in School." *Principal* 76, no. 2 (1996): 22–24.

26. R. DeVries and B. Zan, *Moral Classrooms, Moral Children* (New York, NY: Teachers College Press, 1994).

27. T. Good and G. Brophy, *Looking in Classrooms,* 8th ed. (New York, NY: Longman, 2000), 291.

28. D. W. Johnson, R. T. Johnson, E. J. Holubec, and P. Roy, *Circles of Learning: Cooperation in the Classroom* (Alexandria, VA: Association for Supervision and Curriculum Development, 1984).

29. T. Gordon, *T.E.T.—Teacher Effectiveness Training* (New York, NY: Peter H. Wyden, 1974).

30. P. Drucker, *Post-Capitalist Society* (New York, NY: HarperCollins, 1993), 109, 171.

31. Center for Civic Education, *The Role of Civic Education: A Report of the Task Force on Civic Education* (Calabasas, CA: Author, 1995), 10.

32. E. Schaps and C. Lewis, "Breeding Citizenship through Community in School." *Education Digest* 64, no. 1 (1998): 24.

33. R. Salomone, "Education for Democratic Citizenship." *Education Week* 19, no. 2 (2000): 52.

34. E. Sutherland, written communication (2000).

• *Tour Stop 6* •

Training

> *We need to challenge the "one-size-fits-all" mode of formal staff development which traditionally has introduced standardized content to individuals whose teaching experience, expertise, and settings vary widely.*
>
> —Little, 1993

At this tour stop we provide you with samples of successful training strategies we gathered from the research on effective staff development and our experiences training teachers and others in courses, seminars, academies, and workshops. We also describe in-service and staff development ideas for training teachers, counselors, and staff and include lists and surveys for teacher assessment. Training for character education consists of a variety of factors that may be similar to training for other educational reform purposes. However, to become effective as character educators, educators need opportunities to apply solutions to realistic, diverse settings. In a review of the literature and programs, we have not come across a set of training methods designed specifically for character education. Yet, we have found some strategies and guiding principles that are successful and will share those with you at this tour stop.

We recognize, as we are sure that you do, that the teacher makes the difference in all character education efforts. High-quality curriculum materials are important, but curriculum alone will not guarantee that your students will master the outcomes of the program. According to Leming (1999),[1] who has completed comprehensive reviews of the research on character education, the results are always stronger if the curriculum is implemented consistently; he concluded that the key factor in program effectiveness is the teacher.

TYPICAL TRAINING

Traditionally, training for teachers and staff has come in the form of district or school-mandated workshops. Teachers, generally, have voiced their concerns over the years that they have had no input in choosing or designing in-service training programs. When teachers show up, it is typically because they have to—it is required. Teachers feel compelled to participate, without real commitment, and are often reluctant to learn. In traditional staff-development training teachers may be reluctant because the objectives are unclear or unrealistic, or compete with priorities already established by teachers. With traditional forms of staff development there are many barriers to success; for example, there is poor communication from the administration, no plan for follow-up or ongoing support; teachers may not have the prerequisite skills; and/or there may be unrealistic timelines for implementation. These blocks to successful staff development can and must be avoided when it comes to ethics and character.

Lewis (undated article) tells us that "we know what's wrong with traditional professional development—using good teachers in mundane ways that discourage reflection, sharing, or the building of a professional learning community. It rewards teachers for coursework that is often unrelated to the classroom . . . ; it tends to reinforce practice rather than change it; and it is so unchallenging that teachers put little stock in it."[2] So, how can you make training more effective? Here are a few sets of principles.

EFFECTIVE TRAINING FOR CHARACTER EDUCATION

 *We need to look at a pedagogy around content and teaching for understanding.*

(S. Robinson, former assistant secretary for research at the USDOE)[3]

For training to be successful, a few basic factors must be considered. We highly recommend that during the planning phase of your character education initiatives, you and the CEC think about training in a personal way by following one rule. We'll call it the "Golden Rule" for training: "Train Others as You Would Like to Be Trained." We suggest the following eight principles:

1. Teachers and staff who will engage in the training need to be committed to it (see the "consensus-building" activity at Tour Stop 2).

2. Have teachers and staff participate in goal setting prior to implementing staff development sessions (see the "expectation setting" activity at Tour Stop 2).
3. Communicate! Communicate! Communicate! Communicate often and clearly via memos, e-mail, newsletters, and through Web-discussion.
4. Form small groups for generating plans of action to follow during the implementation phase.
5. Build the plan of action around the strengths within the school, including the expertise of teachers and staff, and the use of community resources.
6. Provide opportunities for teachers and staff to have input and a safe environment to discuss concerns.
7. Supply models and exemplars of the program or activities that work effectively in other settings (see Tour Stop 7).
8. Strategically place supporters in groups to ensure that there is at least one professional in each group who is committed to the success of the character education program. In fact, assigning roles/responsibilities to each group member helps to keep people actively involved and is more likely to lead to positive outcomes.

These principles go along with William Glasser's[4] idea, that if we applied the Golden Rule to teaching/learning, it would be something like: "Teach others as you would want them to teach you." So, the question for teachers doing character education is: "How would you want to be taught/treated if you were a student in class?" The response would probably be something like the following: to be treated kindly and fairly, to be supported, and to be engaged in learning content related to something you feel is important. From the student's point of view, the Golden Rule could be stated as: "Teach me so that I can learn as much as you would learn if you were me." We recommend that teachers try to remember what it is like to be a student, think about how they would like to be treated as a student, and treat their own students that way; in other words, "practice what they preach."

TRAINING THAT REALLY MATTERS

Achieving consensus on a clear vision, and the values that form its foundation, is one of the most powerful ways to build group cohesion around a new course of action.

(Moffett, 1995)[5]

As it is with any change, you cannot make people become effective character educators, just as you cannot mandate what matters for other people. What really matters for achieving the complex goals of character education? According to Michael Fullan (1993),[6] what matters for anything of significance are new skills, creative thinking, internal motivation, and commitment to take action. Just as with children, adults cannot be forced to take on a new attitude or apply a certain strategy. Learning how to be an effective character educator requires being a role model and a willingness to take responsibility for children's character development. To fulfill these two purposes, training needs to go beyond awareness and have more depth than most skills-training workshops.

What Factors Make Staff Development/Training Effective?

Some additional factors have emerged from the research to provide a foundation for effective staff development that goes beyond awareness-level workshops and provides more depth than technical training models. To do that, we recommend that you apply the principles provided in the following two models to training sessions for character education.

Bridges (1991)[7] suggests that effective leaders use what he simply calls the four Ps:

1. *Purpose:* Provide a rationale.
2. *Picture:* Paint a picture of how the program will look.
3. *Plan:* Lay out a step-by-step plan for implementation.
4. *Part:* Give each person a role in the process.

After a review of new studies of professional development and a synthesis of the research, Hawley and Valli (1996)[8] identify eight characteristics of effective professional development:

1. Is driven by analyses of data that show the gap between the goals set for student learning and actual student performance.
2. Involves teachers in the identification of their learning needs.
3. Is primarily school-based and integral to school operations.
4. Provides learning opportunities that relate to individual needs and are ... organized around collaborative problem solving.
5. Is continuous and ongoing, involving follow-up and support for further learning.
6. Uses multiple measures to determine the effect on student outcomes.

7. Provides opportunities to develop a theoretical understanding of the knowledge and skills to be learned.
8. Is integrated with a comprehensive change process that is designed to overcome the barriers to student learning.

Choose whichever set of guiding principles works for you, or take a little bit from each of the models presented. The bottom line: to learn anything new, educators need opportunities to engage in meaningful discussion, to identify problems, and to analyze solutions. As stated previously, for teachers to become effective character educators, opportunities must exist for them to apply creative solutions to realistic problems in diverse settings. We have found case studies, simulations, and Socratic seminars to be three of the most effective methods for training educators because they require participants to apply ethical decision-making and critical-thinking skills to analyze value priorities from multiple perspectives in realistic contexts.

PROMISING FACTORS FOR PROFESSIONAL DEVELOPMENT

Training for character education has not had great success. Most training that we are aware of falls short, in that it is too little, too late, and for too short of a period of time. In the area of character, we cannot afford ineffective training programs. According to Birman, Desimone, Porter, and Baret (2000), six factors emerged from a research study that show the most promise for effective professional development. We have developed an outline for a staff-development plan based on their factors. First we will briefly explain each factor, then provide an example of how the factors can be embedded into a training program for character education to ensure its effectiveness. The authors proposed both structural and process features for effective professional development/training workshops.[9]

STRUCTURAL FEATURES

Form: Is this a traditional workshop or presentation, or is it structured as a "reform" activity (study group, network, task force or committee, action research project, or internship)?

Duration: What are the hours involved and time span for support and follow up?

Participation: Do groups of teachers come from the same school, department, or grade level, or do teachers participate individually from different schools?

PROCESS FEATURES

Content focus: To what degree do the activities focus on deepening and expanding teachers' knowledge about how people learn values and ethics and develop character?

Active learning: What opportunities do teachers have to become actively engaged in meaningful analysis of ethics and character, and effective teaching/learning contexts for character education?

Coherence: Is continued professional communication among educators encouraged, and is the content/process of the sessions aligned with state standards and assessments?

We took Birman et al.'s idea and use it as a template to provide a "road map" for a staff development workshop for character education that follows.

 The formula for success is: be specific and be explicit . . . Or, subordinate the learner to the steps he must take to attain expertise.

(Bruner, 1985)[10]

ROAD MAP: CHARACTER EDUCATION STAFF DEVELOPMENT WORKSHOP

Form: Workshops that are structured as "reform" rather than "traditional" activities work best for character education. Why? As stated earlier, traditional activities do not engage teachers in enough depth. Some examples of reform activities that we have applied successfully are

   a. study groups: teachers read character education books, pamphlets, and articles; view videos; or check Web sites; then discuss their ideas;
   b. networks: teachers engage in local and national discussions, forums, and academies;
   c. task force or committee: teachers join the CEC, CEET, curriculum committee, or district character education task force;

d. action research project: teachers conduct surveys, create lessons, apply ideas they have learned in academies and workshops, then assess the project's impact on students, seeking feedback for improvement;
   e. internship: similar to action research, teachers work more formally in their own school or in others within the district to help others create lessons, apply ideas and methods, and assess the impact on student learning.

Duration: For purposes other than awareness building, the number of hours in training needs to be more than what is typically allocated for staff development workshops. Staff development cannot work in a Wednesday morning three-hour session or a Friday afternoon two-hour session. We have found one-day workshops can be effective *if* they are followed up periodically with more in-depth workshops and ongoing teacher support. We have found that intensive two- to three-day academies or seminars help to build the base of content knowledge required, because they give teachers opportunities to apply the processes that model the ones that teachers will use in their classrooms with their students.

We recommend strongly that if you are going to embark on a character education training program, you prepare for and plan to include the resources necessary for follow-up sessions and ongoing support for teachers as they apply the approaches and strategies. Training programs need to be sustained long enough to allow for lasting results.

Participation: We recommend three different levels of group participation in staff development sessions. You need to choose the level of participation you believe will be most beneficial for your staff, based on your needs and access to resources.

   a. For an individual school's on-site staff development needs, the most efficient and effective training programs require the participation of groups of teachers from the same school, department, or grade level.
   b. When offered off site (district or county level), we recommend you use a "train the trainer" model and send teachers who will participate in clusters or small groups from different schools and then be expected to return to your school and train others.
   c. At a state, regional, or national level seminar or course of study, we recommend that you again use the trainer model. You can send

representative teachers, curriculum coordinators, or staff developers to be trained in character education content and methods. These participants can then train your school staff.

Content focus: The depth and breadth of the training program's content for character education is crucial. Character education content should be integrated into the life and fabric of the school and classroom activities, regardless of the content or activity. Teachers, counselors, and staff need enough depth to know about child-development principles, so that they fully understand how children learn values and ethics and develop character.

Active learning: There are many ways to engage educators in meaningful learning experiences. After examining and trying out some of the best strategies from the adult learning and educational psychology field, we can report great success with the use of case studies, role-plays, simulations, Socratic seminars, action plans, and a hands-on review of curriculum and materials. We also found that these classroom strategies foster outcomes that match up with character education goals and objectives (see the seven Cs at Tour Stop 5).

Coherence: Coherence is what we often see missing in traditional staff development programs because they support unconnected training workshops for individual teachers, with little follow-up or support. In addition to ongoing support and training sessions at regular intervals, as stated earlier, we strongly recommend building school- and district-wide support networks around your character education mission and goals. You should encourage teachers, counselors, and staff developers to join in local study groups, state forums, and regional and national conferences. Continued professional communication among educators should be encouraged.

The content/process of the staff development sessions should link up with and be aligned to state standards and assessments. We all know that what gets assessed, gets taught (see Tour Stop 9). Knowing this, it is important for you to find programs that have aligned themselves to your state's standards and assessments. For example, the Child Development Project[11] and the Heartwood Ethics Curriculum[12] can be linked to content standards in California.

Our purpose for presenting the previous road map is to encourage you to create and endorse staff development for character education that is more likely to create meaningful and lasting results for teachers, counselors, and other staff. Real commitment to implementing character education into classroom and school-wide activities only comes after educators feel comfortable and confident and receive feedback about positive results. We strongly recommend that the CEC provide ongoing mentoring and support for all staff. Researchers at Stanford University and Columbia University Teachers College[13] recommend the following policies that enable schools to get positive results:

- ☐ redesign school structures to support teacher learning and collaboration to give serious attention to practice;
- ☐ rethink schedules and staffing patterns to create blocks of time for teachers to work together and plan;
- ☐ organize the school into small, collaborative groups;
- ☐ make it possible for teachers to think in terms of shared problems, not "my classroom" or "my subject";
- ☐ consider using peer review rather than standard hierarchical supervision; and
- ☐ include everyone in a school community, such as administrators, counselors, staff, and parents in creating a shared purpose/vision.

In order to maintain lasting changes in teacher behaviors, other changes should be made simultaneously. For example, teacher evaluation must be consistent with the roles/responsibilities of teachers. If character education is embedded in teacher evaluation, it is much more likely to be successful.

TEACHER COMPETENCY

You can tie things together by finding a way to assess the competence of your teachers as character educators. To this end, we present you with a teaching-evaluation standards checklist to use when observing classroom teachers. This checklist is based on teaching standards[14] we developed through workshops, academies, seminars, and courses that were found to be helpful as a guide for classroom teachers. We encourage you to share them with teachers and then use them as a way to informally assess each teacher's competence as a character educator.

Teacher Evaluation Standards Checklist

☐ STANDARD 1: This teacher is observed to practice and reflect on his/her role and responsibilities as a character educator.

☐ STANDARD 2: The teacher demonstrates understanding of his/her role and responsibilities as a value transmitter and role model and communicates high expectations for all students regarding pro-social behaviors. It is evident that he or she strives, along with students, to eliminate behaviors that are antithetical to good character.

☐ STANDARD 3: The teacher creates a classroom climate that emulates mutual trust and respect and supports the tenets of a community of learners (e.g., caring and cooperative).

☐ STANDARD 4: The teacher engages all students in ethical analysis, critical inquiry, and higher-order thinking skills as they pursue ethical dilemmas in the content areas (e.g., literature, history, health, media, and life skills) and co-curricular activities.

☐ STANDARD 5: The teacher develops lessons that provide students with positive value experiences and opportunities to practice applying core values.

☐ STANDARD 6: Knowing that the community, peer groups, and the media have a major influence on the character development of the young, the teacher forms collaborative partnerships between home, school, and the community that welcome and involve others in character-development efforts.

E	M	N
Exceeds expectations	Meets expectations	Needs improvement

Comments: _____

You, or the CEC, can help teachers to be more effective by using checklists/surveys like this one. We have added other checklists throughout the book that will help you to examine teacher attributes and competencies (see Tour Stop 5), gather student information (see Tour Stop 9), and recommend instructional strategies (like the seven Cs). The checklists/surveys are designed to help teachers reach character education goals.

We want to share a checklist for constructivist teaching that can be helpful as teachers plan lessons. We use this checklist in training sessions, so that teachers have a guide for planning and implementing lessons. Teachers should check to see if their lesson

- ☐ emphasizes learning and not teaching;
- ☐ encourages and accepts learner autonomy and initiative;
- ☐ sees learners as creatures of will and purpose;
- ☐ thinks of learning as a process;
- ☐ encourages learner inquiry;
- ☐ acknowledges the crucial role of experience in learning;
- ☐ nurtures learners' natural curiosity;
- ☐ takes the learner's mental model into account;
- ☐ encourages self-awareness or reflective practice of the knowledge-construction process;
- ☐ emphasizes performance and understanding when assessing learning;
- ☐ bases itself on the principles of the cognitive theory;
- ☐ makes extensive use of cognitive terminology such as predict, create, and analyze;
- ☐ considers how the student learns;
- ☐ encourages learners to engage in dialogue with other students and with the teacher;
- ☐ supports cooperative learning;
- ☐ involves learners in real-world, relevant situations;
- ☐ emphasizes the context in which learning takes place, appreciates multiple perspectives;
- ☐ considers the beliefs and attitudes of the learner; and
- ☐ provides learners with the opportunity to construct new knowledge and understanding from authentic experience

STUDENT INFORMATION

Many educators are re-discovering an historic truth, that good character and good learning complement each other.

(Wynne, 1998)[15]

As a "tour thought," we believe that it is essential for educators to gather information about what students know and are thinking about values, ethics, and civic behavior. The CEC, school administrators, and teachers should gather baseline information about students' thoughts and behaviors before starting and during character education initiatives. The CEC should take the pulse of the students in this area before implementing action plans with curricular and co-curricular activities. We encourage you to find and use a survey (see Tour Stop 9) for the students in your school (the survey may need adjustments/adaptations for use with elementary, middle, and high school students). The same survey can be used as a pre/post assessment for students at benchmark grade levels over a number of years (e.g., K–2, 3–5, 7–9, and 10–12). The survey can give you information about children's feelings about and applications of the values that they believe are important. The results gathered from different surveys, administered periodically, can be an invaluable tool for communicating with stakeholders and parents about what the children think, know, and can do. The information is invaluable for guiding teachers as they plan lessons, for you as you develop school-wide activities, and for advising the CEC as it assesses the program's effectiveness.

Educational psychologists say educators need to know what their students' prior knowledge is—that is, students' background knowledge—so they can use it as a baseline for preparing lessons and activities. The information generated from a student survey will help teachers, in particular, prepare more appropriate lessons and activities for character development.

TEACHER SELF-ASSESSMENT

Student learning and teaching are two sides of the same coin—they need to be in sync. Reflection through self-assessment is particularly helpful because it enables teachers to understand student perceptions and how teacher behavior impacts students. We put together the following teacher self-assessment checklist that can be used for reflection on practice. This assessment is based upon Williams' study related to students' perceptions about the attributes of the teachers whom they "respect."[16]

Teacher Self-Assessment

- ☐ Creates a community of learners/a supportive, collaborative climate;
- ☐ Provides an environment that fosters mutual respect and trust;
- ☐ Listens;
- ☐ Asks questions that enable students to develop critical-thinking skills;

☐ Welcomes student questions;
☐ Challenges students with engaging learning activities;
☐ Utilizes learning activities that promote character development (e.g., conflict resolution, cooperative learning, class meetings, critical thinking, etc.);
☐ Attends to student concerns—really cares about student learning;
☐ Models the behavior students are asked to follow;
☐ Works hard;
☐ Establishes and maintains positive working relationships with parents;
☐ Is available for students outside of class time; and
☐ Includes student input/choice in content-learning activities

AN EVALUATION IDEA FOR TEACHERS

In addition to teacher self-assessment, we propose a checklist to identify items that teachers know about and do related to character education. You, or the CEC, can use the Teacher Planning Guide to work with individual teachers or groups of teachers as a way to begin action plans and lesson plans for teaching the core values.

Teacher Planning Guide for Character Education

The teacher:

___ has a relationship with students;
___ has a relationship with parents
___ has strategies to work with parents;
___ collaborates with colleagues in the school;
___ has knowledge of moral education and character development;
___ is able to implement the core values into the classroom climate;
___ is able to maintain and audit a classroom climate that supports character development;
___ is able to implement the core values into the curriculum, maximize opportunities to learn;
___ helps students build intrinsic motivation to learn;
___ uses the seven Cs: connections, constructivism, classroom management, critical thinking, conflict resolution, cooperative learning, and citizenship;

___ has high expectations for student learning, yet minimizes student frustration by using a mastery approach;
___ uses effective classroom management and has a sense of efficacy;
___ has access to materials for use in teaching the core values;
___ has received training in using character education strategies and materials; and
___ is aware of the attributes of effective character educators (see Tour Stop 5).

There is a pressing need for teachers to understand how to integrate character education into lessons. In our fast-paced, standards-driven era of accountability, the teaching of values often gets ignored or left out, because teachers do not know where and how to fit it into already very busy schedules. What teachers need most are ideas and sample strategies of how to infuse character education into classroom processes, across all content areas. Good and Brophy[17] describe the key to effective teaching as teacher decision making—guided by clear goals. Teachers have a role/responsibility in actively presenting information to students, involving and engaging them in activities and assignments, and adapting their approach to the individual differences of students.

ASSESSMENT EXAMPLE: STRATEGIES IMPACT PERCEPTIONS

Suppose the CEC or CEET is interested in determining how teachers view a range of teaching/learning strategies that in some schools are the core of the character education program. To do this, a scale, similar to the following, might be helpful.

Directions: The purpose of this scale is to gauge the probable impact of the following strategies on a school's character education program, some of which may or may not occur in our program. We would appreciate your opinion of the probable impact of each item. Circle the letter after each item. Return the completed scale to the school secretary or to a member of CEET.

Element Impact	High	Moderate	Low
1. Cooperative learning	H	M	L
2. Service learning	H	M	L
3. Value-a-month program	H	M	L

4. Posters	H	M	L
5. Literature	H	M	L
6. Rewards/recognition program	H	M	L
7. Discussion of values	H	M	L
8. Co-curricular program	H	M	L
9. Student activities program	H	M	L
10. Conflict resolution	H	M	L
11. Violence-prevention program	H	M	L
12. Peer mediation	H	M	L
13. Problem-centered learning	H	M	L
14. Staff development	H	M	L
15. Support by administration	H	M	L
16. Parent involvement	H	M	L
17. Community support	H	M	L
18. Critical thinking emphasis	H	M	L
19. Substance abuse program	H	M	L
20. High expectations of students	H	M	L
21. Teachers who care	H	M	L
22. Parental support	H	M	L
23. Student participation	H	M	L
24. Central office support	H	M	L

    a. Which three items do you feel the CEC should attend to immediately? Write the numbers here: ___ ___ ___
    b. Which three items would you like more information about? ___ ___ ___
    c. Which three items should be the basis of staff development meetings? ___ ___ ___
    d. Which three items should be evaluated soon? ___ ___ ___

TOUR THOUGHTS

Many more assessment instruments can be used by teachers, principals, and central office personnel to assess the effectiveness of teaching for character, teaching the core values of the program. At this tour stop our main goal was to provide you with a strong rationale for staff development and training programs that link up with current recommendations for reform in staff development practices. At the next tour stop we share our tips and ideas about character education programs, curriculum, and school-wide and student activity programs.

A NOTE ABOUT COLLEGIALITY

Staff development specialists recommend implementing special institutes and courses that offer teachers substantive depth and focus; adequate time to grapple with ideas and materials; the sense of doing "real" work rather than being "talked at;" and opportunities to consult with colleagues and experts (Little, 1993). "Research reveals that the most successful learning does, in fact, occur in schools where teachers not only teach skillfully in separate classrooms, but also find solutions together."[18] Collegiality is an essential ingredient of teacher effectiveness that is rarely addressed in schools. Time does not usually permit cooperation and collaboration among teachers. Yet, the more teachers in your school have an opportunity to work together on lessons, activities, curricular and co-curricular plans, partnership activities, and school-wide events, the stronger the character education program will be and the more successful students will be in learning the core values.

THE INTERNATIONAL CENTER FOR CHARACTER EDUCATION, UNIVERSITY OF SAN DIEGO

We are in San Diego. Our tour bus enters the beautiful campus of the University of San Diego. We are dropped off at the fountain in the center of campus. There is a bright blue sky and the sun is shimmering off the waters of the fountain, as a gentle breeze blows in from the ocean, which we can see in the distance. We, the authors, take you on a tour of the campus, which concludes with lunch on the patio in the Rose Garden.

We then go to the Manchester Executive Conference Center's auditorium for a program about the work of the International Center for Character Education (ICCE). We are greeted and welcomed by the president of the university, the dean of the school of education, and the director of the division of continuing education.

Mary begins with a short presentation about ICCE, how it was conceived and developed over the years. She continues by describing the yearly conference and academy format and some of the speakers we have had. A videotape is played, showing the presentations of a sample of keynote speakers. She discusses the history of ICCE and the ICCE mission, which is to: "enable school personnel, parents, teacher educators, faith community members, youth providers, and concerned individuals to come together to ... study, discuss, learn, practice, reflect, and write on issues, programs, problems, and promises regarding the character education of children and youth."[19] The ICCE's focus is on the four pillars of democracy: home, school, church (faith community), and community. And, the ICCE's purpose is to train educators and community members to be effective with character education initiatives.

Ed talks about the outreach programs of the ICCE, describing the workshops and seminars held for educators throughout California and around the United States. He tells about the presentations both have made throughout this country and internationally, and why we have done so. We are strongly committed to carrying out the ICCE mission and feel that by working with people (principals, teachers, counselors, parents, and community members), we can have an impact on future generations.

Mary returns to talk about the development of a character education certificate program and a master's degree specialization in character education for graduate students. She notes that the numerous inquiries regarding further training compelled us to create a program whereby educators could gain greater expertise regarding character education and ultimately be seen as specialists in their school and district. Thus, the Certificate in Character Education Program was launched. With the increasing number of inquiries from educators across the country, we decided that we could serve the needs of more people by going online with the certificate program. On-LineLearning.net took on the task of providing the platform for learning that allowed us to begin training educators across the country and around the world. Simultaneously, knowing that the research on the effectiveness of character education programs and practices is slim and that there will be a growing need for greater specialization in this area, we received approval for an M.Ed. specialization in character education (the first of its kind in the country).

Ed narrates segments of a videotape showing participants in class completing case studies, discussing strategies for implementing character education in their schools, and assessing curricular materials using our curriculum standards. These are the teachers and other educators who are earning a certificate in character education (the first program of its kind in the country). Ed then introduces three of the teachers to our group. Each of the three, representing different school levels, talks about what he or she has learned and how he or she has implemented character education in the classroom and the school.

Our campus tour ends in late afternoon. The bus will now take us to the famous San Diego Zoo for an early evening dinner and an opportunity to visit the animals.

T. Devine, J. H. Seuk, and A. Wilson, *Cultivating Heart and Character: Educating for Life's Most Essential Goals* (Chapel Hill, NC: Character Development Publishing, 2000).

J. L. Goodlad, R. Soder, and K. Sirotnik, eds., *The Moral Dimensions of Teaching* (San Francisco, CA: Jossey-Bass, 1990).

H. Kirschenbaum, *100 Ways to Enhance Values and Morality in School and Youth Settings* (Boston, MA: Allyn & Bacon, 1995).

The Center for the 4th and 5th R's, *http://www.cortland.edu/www/c4n5rs*.
The Council for Global Education, *http://www.globaleducation.org*.
The School for Ethical Education, *http://www.ethicsed.org*.

REFERENCES

1. J. S. Leming, "Current Evidence Regarding Program Effectiveness in Character Education: A Brief Review." In M. Williams and E. Schaps, eds., *Character Education: The Foundation for Teacher Education* (Washington, DC: Character Education Partnership, 1999), 53.

2. A. C. Lewis, "A New Consensus Emerges on the Characteristics of Good Professional Development." In *The Best of the Harvard Education Letter: Meeting the Challenges of Reform* (Cambridge, MA: Harvard Education Publishing Group), 6.

3. S. Robinson, former assistant secretary for research at the USDOE, in A. C. Lewis, "A New Consensus Emerges on the Characteristics of Good Professional Development." In *The Best of the Harvard Education Letter: Meeting the Challenges of Reform* (Cambridge, MA: Harvard Education Publishing Group).

4. W. Glasser, *The Quality School: Managing Students without Coercion* (New York, NY: HarperCollins, 1985).

5. C. Moffett, "Resistance to Change: Taking a Closer Look." *Professional Development Newsletter* (Alexandria, VA: Association for Supervision and Curriculum Development, 1995), 8.

6. M. Fullan, "Innovation, Reform, and Restructuring Strategies." In G. Gawelti, ed., *ASCD 1993 Yearbook: Challenges and Achievements of American Education* (Alexandria, VA: Association for Supervision and Curriculum Development, 1993).

7. W. Bridges, *Managing Transitions* (Boston, MA: Addison-Wesley, 1991).

8. W. Hawley and L. Valli, "The Essentials of Effective Professional Development: A New Consensus" (paper presented at the AERA Invitational Conference on Teacher Development and School Reform, Washington, DC, 1996).

9. B. F. Birman, L. Desimone, A. C. Porter, and M. S. Baret, "Designing Professional Development That Works." *Educational Leadership* 8, no. 57 (2000): 29.

10. J. Bruner, "Models of the Learner" (paper presented as an Invited Address at the AERA Annual Conference, Chicago, IL, 1985).

11. The Child Development Project, *http//www.devstu.org*.

12. The Heartwood Ethics Curriculum, *http//www.enviroweb.org/heartwood*.

13. L. Darling-Hammond and M. McLaughlin, "Policies That Support Professional Development in an Era of Reform." In M. McLaughlin and I. Oberman, eds., *Teacher Learning: New Policy, New Practices* (New York, NY: Teachers College Press, 1996).

14. E. F. DeRoche and M. M. Williams, *Educating Hearts and Minds: A Comprehensive Character Education Program,* 2d ed. (Thousand Oaks, CA: Corwin Press, 2001).

15. E. A. Wynne, "Looking at Good Schools." In K. Ryan and J. Cooper, eds., *Kaleidoscope: Readings in Education* (Boston, MA: Houghton Mifflin, 1998), 201–209.

16. M. M. Williams, "Actions Speak Louder Than Words: What Students Think about Character Education." *Educational Leadership* (November 1993).

17. T. L. Good, and J. E. Brophy, *Looking in Classrooms,* 8th ed. (New York, NY: Longman, 2000).

18. E. L. Boyer, *The Basic School: A Community for Learning* (Princeton, NJ: The Carnegie Foundation for the Advancement of Teaching, 1995), 35.

19. International Center for Character Education Web site, *http://teachvalues.org*.

• *Tour Stop 7* •

Programs

Sports do not build character. They reveal it.

—Heywood Hale Broun

We admit that you could see many more things at this "tour stop," but our tour time limits us to four character education attractions (programs): school-wide activities, student-activity programs, service-learning programs, and curricular and intervention programs. At each attraction, our intent is to offer enough information and suggestions so that you and the school's CEC can plan accordingly.

SCHOOL-WIDE ACTIVITIES

The mission and goals are in place. The core values have been agreed upon and defined. The school climate, leadership, and teaching methods are ready. So, let the programs and activities begin. We suggest that the CEC start with an examination of school-wide activities. Our view is that the school climate must be such that when the stakeholders are ready to implement character education initiatives, the environment will be receptive and supportive. The climate of the school has to be inviting, supportive, and encouraging (see Tour Stop 4).

Following are a few examples of school-wide activities:

- special programs (drug use and abuse, parenting programs, conflict resolution)

112 Tour Stop 7

- activities (assemblies, public announcements, tutoring, school-wide projects)
- staff and administrator behaviors (role modeling, counseling, coaching, mentoring)
- policies (discipline, behaviors, rights and responsibilities, rules and procedures handbook)
- celebrations (recognition of students and school personnel for exemplary work, behavior, and contributions)
- citizenship (community service learning projects)

You will recall that we listed fifty ways to improve the school climate through character education initiatives at Tour Stop Four. We also included ways for the CEC to evaluate the existing school climate. We urge you to revisit that "tour stop" as the forerunner to implementing the ideas that we are about to share regarding student activities, service learning, and curriculum.

The major point here is that school-wide activities should be an essential part of the school's character education efforts.

The No. 1 goal of high school activity programs is the propagation of good people—good citizens who will contribute to the quality of life in the U.S. and around the world.

(Kanaby, 1996)[1]

STUDENT-ACTIVITIES PROGRAM

Call it what you will—the co-curricular program, the extracurricular program, the paracurriculum—the student-activities program is a major contributor to meeting the mission and expectations of the school's character education initiatives. The values and benefits of the student-activities program are too great to ignore. Therefore, debate teams; academic, vocational, and service clubs; student government; student publications; the performing arts program; and sports offer opportunities that should involve most, if not all, of the students in your school. In many ways, it is in these programs that values such as respect, responsibility, courage, persistence, patience, honesty, fair play, and courtesy are developed.

In fact, one could make a solid argument that if schools, particularly high schools, are going to have students complete a service-learning requirement, they should be required to participate in at least one of the school's student-activities programs because the benefits are well documented. The CEC should make the facts known and use them as a way to promote greater student participation in school activities. Here are two examples.

NASSP's Department of Student Activities (1997) reports that students involved in student activities in middle schools:

- have higher achievement;
- have better attendance;
- are less likely to experiment with drugs or participate in illicit behaviors; and
- are likely to continue to be active in high school, college, and beyond.

An excerpt from the report *Breaking Ranks*[2] says that U. S. Department of Education research studies show that students who participate in cocurricular activities have more consistent attendance, better academic achievement, and higher aspirations; are less likely to use drugs; and are less likely to drop out of school than nonparticipants. In addition, Holloway's[3] review of the research reveals that

- gifted students tend to spend "extra" time in student organizations;
- at-risk students benefit from such programs because these programs develop the student–school connection;
- academic achievement of students participating in athletics is not endangered and may be enhanced by such participation;
- activities programs increase connections between the students and the school and its values; and
- extracurricular activities provide all students—including at-risk and gifted students—with an academic safety net.

Students' opportunities to participate in the school's activities program vary according to school level, size, resources, and, at least in sports, the student's grade point average. So, the roles and responsibilities of the CEC will be different at each school, much easier in elementary schools and more complex in secondary schools, where the activities program offers students a range of options. The values and tenets of the character education initiatives should permeate the school culture. It should be found in all programs, formal and informal, hidden and explicit. Therefore, in our opinion, the CEC should have some input in the student-activities program, particularly the sports programs.

What we are getting at is the administrative arrangement between two programs. The problems of who is responsible to whom and how the programs are related seem less likely to be issues in elementary schools. They are issues that secondary school administrators have to address. Since there is such a variation in middle and high schools because of size, resources, and offerings, there can be no single answer. But you and the stakeholders in your school must agree to an administrative arrangement because, at some point, issues and problems of jurisdiction may arise. They will certainly be of interest to all parties when the CEET decides to "evaluate" the student-activities program regarding the program's contribution to the expectations and outcomes of the school's character education initiatives.

There are five key questions for the CEC:

1. How does the student-activities program contribute to the mission and expectations of the school's character education efforts?
2. Are the purposes of the student-activities program aligned with the intent of the school's character education initiatives?
3. Do the outcomes of the student-activities program match and support outcomes for character education?
4. Are the core values of the school taught, fostered, and promoted in the student-activities program?
5. Is there a plan to regularly evaluate each of the activities offered by the school in relation to its contributions to the school's character education initiatives?

SERVICE LEARNING

Service is the rent we pay for living.

Marian Wright Edelman, Children's Defense Fund

You have probably read and heard much about the purposes of and benefits from schools' service-learning projects. Rifkin[4] summarizes it nicely when he says that "service learning is an essential antidote to the increasingly isolated world of simulation and virtual reality children experience in the classroom and at home in front of the television and at their computer workstations."

In the character education arena, some have engaged in a debate about whether service learning is character education or whether character education must include service learning. A school can have a service-learning program without having a character education program. Many do, but our view is that it would be best for students and the school's stakeholders if the character education program was the "umbrella" for the service learning program, particularly for organizational purposes as outlined in the components of the framework. We feel that service learning and intervention programs the school may sponsor are best implemented within the character education framework.

Service learning takes various forms in schools. Some schools arrange community-service activities for which their students volunteer. Other schools have established a certain number of hours of service learning as part of their graduation requirements. Some schools have students go out into the community and find their own community-service projects. Other schools arrange projects for students. There are also schools that do not have a mandated or volunteer community-service program. Our position is that "service"

1. should be a part of a school's character education program;
2. should begin at home, continue at school, and then be expanded into the community;
3. should encompass both volunteerism and requirements; and
4. that home, school, and community projects should be created by students and their teachers and by other adults at the school and in the community.

For purposes of this discussion, we are going to assume that the CEC has support from its stakeholders to include the concept and practice of "service" in its character education efforts. That being the case, the following guidelines are offered to the CEC. We call them the "Six Ps for Service Learning" in your school.

Purpose: Yes, there must be a purpose to service learning in your school. What is it? Does it emanate from, or reflect, the mission, expectations, and core values of the character education program?

Possibilities: It may be that the school's service-learning program may help students make connections between service and

- what they are learning in the classroom;
- other aspects of the school's character education program;
- the ethic of caring and community;
- skill development and skill application;

- school and careers;
- citizenship;
- teamwork; and
- the Golden Rule.

Principles: An effective service-learning program in your school results by applying the following principles:

- students have a voice in plans and actions;
- the school works closely with organizations to meet the needs of both;
- teachers are trained and students are prepared for their work;
- resources are available to meet needs;
- evaluation occurs on a regular basis;
- all partners are committed to the success of the program; and
- service is seen as part of the school's character education efforts.

Personnel: The CEC and you have to decide who will be responsible for the service-learning program. Will it be a newly hired coordinator? Will a teacher be given release time to coordinate the program? Will a volunteer administer it? Will the responsibility be assumed by CEC? Or, will you take it on as another of your administrative tasks?

Projects: The CEC should strongly suggest to the stakeholders that the service-learning program begin with teacher-created and student-created projects that meet needs at home, in classrooms, and in the school. After teachers and students have had some success with these projects, the CEC can then expand the program into the community.

Pride: It is hoped that the program evaluation will reveal compelling testimonials about the work students have done. There will be stories to tell the community and articles for the school newspaper. The students will show pride in their service work. The recipients of the service will express pleasure in having students in their homes, at their agencies, or at their workplaces. This "pride" in the program should be made public.

Two Examples

Two award-winning schools offer us examples of how school-community service projects foster the values of good character at an elementary and a high school.

At Newsome Park Elementary (Newport News, VA) community service is central to the school's character education program. Students learn about community issues, learn about the action they can take and how to apply the values of responsibility, courage, kindness, and respect. In cooperation with the Department of Social Services, students participate in an "adopt-a-family" program as well as an "adopt-a-ward" project in the local VA hospital. Teachers take the younger students on field trips into the community under a program titled "How Things Work."[5]

At Pattonville High School (Maryland Heights, MO) students run their own credit union in conjunction with the local employee's credit union. The STARS (Students Taking Action Reaching Students) Project offers students the opportunity to work with at-risk elementary and middle school students. Commitment and reflection underscore a fifty-hour community-service graduation requirement in which all students participate in community-service activities. The district funds the cost of a full-time community-service coordinator and pays the transportation cost for ninth graders to do a full-day community project, such as working in gardens, hospitals, homeless shelters, and humane societies.[6]

PROGRAMS

Character education is one of the largest educational reforms currently taking place in P–12 schools. Many programs are springing up, and this makes it difficult to make curricular decisions. Some programs connect with content-area lessons, others contain classroom or school-wide supplemental activity programs, and still others are community-based programs.

Today, more than ever, education represents a moral as well as intellectual investment in our youth . . . [I]t costs little or nothing to infuse core values into every aspect of school life.

(Quinn, 1997)[7]

We have found that the most successful programs are those that mirror/reflect the mission and values of the school, along with the expectations/outcomes that were determined. A coherent match must be made between your school's goals and the goals of the program that you choose to implement (see Curriculum Standards Checklist). Therefore, we recommend that the CEC appoint a subcommittee to work on curriculum and co-curricular activity programs, to analyze and make decisions on curriculum materials and programs for the school's character education initiatives.

CURRICULUM: PROGRAM STANDARDS CHECKLIST

We do not endorse a particular character-education curriculum or program. As we noted earlier, a variety of programs exist under the character-education "umbrella." What is best for your school should be decided by the CEC as it tries to match the program to the school's core values, expectations, and outcomes. To help you decide which program or combination of programs may be best for your school, we propose two checklists.

Program Standards Checklist

The character education curricular program:

- ☐ fosters the core values and matches the expectations and outcomes of the character education program;
- ☐ can be incorporated into, adapted to, or integrated with existing content-area syllabi;
- ☐ is developmentally appropriate and intrinsically motivating, providing rich and varied contexts for students to apply the core values;
- ☐ can easily be adapted and revised to use in a variety of settings, with diverse students;
- ☐ includes a separate teacher guide that has sample daily or unit plans, questions to ask students, classroom activities, strategies for parents, and assessment criteria;
- ☐ promotes critical thinking in students, that is, ethical decision-making and moral-reasoning skills to evaluate problems or issues;
- ☐ requires students to put the core values into practice (e.g., hands-on activities, cooperative group processing with peers, and/or co-curricular activities, such as service learning); and
- ☐ does not contain any materials or references that are biased toward any group—in other words, the authors' perspectives, the packaging of materials, the language and style of the written and graphic materials, and the content.

Rating Scale for Program Standards Checklist

Not recommended: Meets up to two of the standards on the checklist.
Consider: Meets up to four of the standards on the checklist.
Satisfactory: Meets up to six of the standards on the checklist.
Excellent match: Meets all of the standards on the checklist.

We recommend that the CEC use the program standards checklist and rating scale when evaluating a character education curriculum or when creating its own. Finding an "excellent match" between the school's expectations and the curriculum may take time. Time is well spent on curriculum materials, because the curricular vehicle often drives the entire character education program.

In addition to determining the quality and fit of the program by using the standards checklist, the CEC would want a few questions answered that are related to curriculum. How does the curriculum chosen by the group differ from others? Does the curriculum match program goals? Have time and money expended on the curriculum yielded results? How will we evaluate the curriculum's effectiveness in meeting the expectations (or reaching the outcomes) of the program?

CURRICULUM: PROGRAM PRINCIPLES

One final question to answer about curriculum is whether or not it will engage the students in learning the core values. Learning takes place when an activity is perceived by the learner to be rewarding. However, what one student perceives to be of value, another sees as a waste of time. There are some questions you can answer to see if the curriculum has specific appeal to students and will engage them (McNeil).[8]

Curriculum: Program Principles Questions

1. Have the curriculum developers listed prerequisites for each activity?
2. Will the students find the activities satisfying? Some criteria to use:
   a. Hands-on: students enjoy being able to handle objects or construct something.
   b. Challenging: students learn when they are exposed to puzzling situations, when preconceived notions are challenged, when cognitive dissonance is generated.

c. Social: students learn from peers, enjoy working with others on interdependent tasks of mutual interest and concern, and resolve problems.
   d. Holistic: students learn more, in ways that are more powerful and meaningful, when activities tap into the cognitive, affective, and behavioral domains.
3. Does the activity require more competitive or cooperative skills?
4. Is the activity socially oriented or focused on task completion?

In order to make final curricular decisions, we recommend using a set of guiding principles, like the ones we have adapted here from Doll (1992),[9] which are made into a checklist.

Program Principles Checklist

☐ Principle 1: Curriculum decisions should be made for valid educational reasons, to match up with the core values.
☐ Principle 2: Curriculum decisions should be made on the basis of the best available evidence.
☐ Principle 3: Curriculum decisions should be made in a context of the expectations of the character education program.
☐ Principle 4: Curriculum decisions should be made within the context of the school's content standards so that balance may be safeguarded.
☐ Principle 5: Curriculum decisions should be made by achieving a resolution of forces originating in the nature and development of ethics and values in learners, the goals of the local community, and the nature and structure of character education content.
☐ Principle 6: Curriculum decisions should be reached cooperatively by stakeholders legitimately involved in the effects of the decisions.
☐ Principle 7: Curriculum decisions should take into account new facts of human life such as the proliferation of knowledge and a need for a new sense of unity within our diversity.
☐ Principle 8: Curriculum decisions should take into account the many differences among learners, especially with reference to their potential for development, their styles of thinking, and their need for education in the core values.
☐ Principle 9: Curriculum decisions should be made with a realistic view of all other school factors that can affect the quality of the

decisions themselves—for instance, the distinction between curriculum content and pupils' experiences and the uses of time.
☐ Principle 10: Curriculum decisions should be made with some forethought about ways in which they may be communicated and shared.
☐ Principle 11: Curriculum decisions should be made only with reference to character education content and student experiences that cannot be offered as satisfactorily outside the school.

BASIC PROGRAMS

Several programs have enriched the character education curriculum in elementary, middle, and secondary schools that we think you and the CEC should know about. We have arbitrarily developed two categories for the character education programs that we have reviewed over the years. The first, we will call "basic programs." These are programs that have most, if not all, of the following elements: are comprehensive, are content-based, are recognized by experts in the field to be noteworthy, are supported by educational organizations, and have fairly good research results. We describe seven basic programs in the following section. We define the supplemental programs as those that offer a special emphasis under the character education "umbrella," are specific in content and intent, have fairly good research results, and are generally seen by experts to be "intervention" or supplemental programs.

CHARACTER COUNTS!

The six pillars of character upon which this school-community character education program is based include trustworthiness, respect, responsibility, fairness, caring, and citizenship. Operated by the Josephson Institute of Ethics and endorsed by a large coalition of educational, civic, and youth-serving agencies, program offerings include character-development seminars, community-awareness workshops, educator in-service programs, and training for teachers working with high-risk youth. The institute offers a variety of instructional materials for elementary and middle school educators.

Contact: Josephson Institute, 4640 Admiralty Way #1001, Marina del Rey, CA 90292-6610; Tel: (800) 711-2670; Web site: *http://www.charactercounts.org*.

CHARACTER EDUCATION INSTITUTE

This institute offers P–9 educators a "Character Education Curriculum," which includes instructional kits for P–6 grade teachers and one kit for 7–9 grade teachers. The kits include topical lessons and student activities focusing on good self-esteem, responsibility, drug prevention, self-discipline, critical thinking, decision making, resisting negative peer pressure, respect, accepting individual differences, cooperative learning, and economic security. Teacher in-service programs are provided by the staff and consultants.

Contact: 8918 Tesoro Drive, Suite 575, San Antonio, TX 78217-6253; Tel: (800) 284-0499; Fax: (210) 829-1729; Web site: *http://www.Character Education.org*.

CHILD DEVELOPMENT PROJECT

Probably the best researched and most written about character education program for elementary schools and endorsed by the National Association of Elementary School Principals is the Child Development Project (CDP). The CDP has three components to its character education program. One is a classroom program that includes a literature-based approach to reading and language arts, coupled with a cooperative learning emphasis and classroom management and discipline practices that develop the class as a caring community of learners. The second program includes an array of school-wide activities and events. The third approach is a family-involvement program that is closely coordinated with the school curriculum and school-wide events. The intent of the program is to create a "caring community of learners" in classrooms and in schools.

Contact: Development Studies Center, 2000 Embarcadero, Suite 305, Oakland, CA 94606-5300; Tel: (510) 533-0213; Fax: (510) 464-3670; Web site: *http://www.devstu.org*.

COMMUNITY OF CARING

This program is a project of the Joseph F. Kennedy, Jr. Foundation and is endorsed by the National Association of Secondary School Principals. The project works to promote and encourage five values in schools, using a total community approach: caring, respect, responsibility, trust, and family. Program offerings include teacher training, student value discussions and forums, family involvement, and community service opportunities for students.

Contact: 1325 G Street, N.W., Washington, DC 20005; Tel: (202) 393-1251; Fax: (202) 824-0351; Web site: *http://www.communityofcaring.org*.

HEARTWOOD ETHICS INSTITUTE

The Heartwood Ethics Institute has a curriculum for elementary school children that is a literature-based character education program. It provides teachers with a multicultural reading kit filled with beautifully written and illustrated books that include folk and hero stories, legends, and contemporary tales. The content of each grade level kit contains seven universal concepts: courage, loyalty, justice, respect, hope, honesty, and love. The kit also includes lesson cards for each book, a resource manual, flags, and a world map addressing the location of each of the stories. Recent research on the effectiveness of the Heartwood Ethics program was conducted by Jim Leming (see *http://www.character.org*.

Contact: 425 N. Craig St., Suite 302, Pittsburgh, PA 15213; Tel: (800) HEART-10; Fax: (412) 688-8552; Web site: *http://www.heartwoodethics.org*.

THE INSTITUTE FOR GLOBAL ETHICS

The Institute for Global Ethics (IGE) vision is for "A world where shared moral values shape relationships, determine decisions, and guide actions for every individual, institution, and nation. The IGE mission is to promote public discourse and practical action around significant ethical issues by: (1) discovering and defining the global common ground of shared values; (2) establishing clear structures for moral reasoning and ethical decision making; (3) promoting the teaching of *ethical fitness* in the practices of private, institutional, and civic virtue; (4) analyzing trends, gathering and disseminating information, and developing new knowledge about global ethics; and (5) being a model organization in effectiveness, outreach, efficiency, and ethical action. The IGE divides its efforts into three primary areas of concern: Corporate Services, Education Programs, and Public Policy Programs. They have an international board of directors, an international advisory council, and a network of nationwide and global connections.

Contact: 11 Main Street, P.O. Box 563, Camden, ME 04843; Tel: (207) 236-6658; Fax: (207) 236-4014; Web site: *http://www.globalethics.org*.

QUEST INTERNATIONAL

Supported by Lions Clubs throughout the world, endorsed by several educational organizations, and with some research support, Quest International (QI) offers a variety of curriculum and instructional materials for teachers and students at all grade levels. The K–5 program is called "Skills for Growing;" 6–8 is "Skills for Adolescence;" and 9–12 is "Skills for Action." Life skills, character education, drug prevention, violence prevention, and service learning are its major emphases. QI offers education professional development workshops, evaluation assistance, and youth advocacy presentations.

Contact: 1984 Coffman Rd., P.O. Box 4850, Newark, OH 43058-4850; Tel: (800) 446-2700; Fax: (410) 522-6580; Web site: *http://www.quest.edu*.

INTERVENTION PROGRAMS

As you look through the tour bus windows, we want to point out that today's schools offer many different types of intervention programs, in addition to curricular programs. While it is not our intent to list what appears to be well over fifty intervention or supplemental programs that we are aware of, we have selected a dozen topics for programs that you and the CEC may want more information about.

- peace education
- drug use/abuse
- peer mediation
- life skills development
- violence prevention
- alcohol use/abuse
- conflict resolution
- social/emotional training
- safety education
- smoking prevention
- leadership training
- self-esteem training

In some schools, programs related to these topics are considered to be supplemental to the school's character education efforts. In other schools, these programs are used to meet short-term, crisis-reaction needs. In a few schools, they are the one and only character education program. These and other intervention efforts come under the character education "umbrella" of initiatives. It is the character education program that will give them purpose and permanence. In our opinion, "supplemental" programs alone cannot meet the expectations for a school's character education efforts. The school's comprehensive character education initiatives give each individual program purpose and permanence. The school's CEC can apply the standards, guiding principles, and evaluation methods described at various tour stops in this book to supplemental programs. You can access more information about intervention programs by searching by topic on the Character Education Partnership Web site at *http://www.character.org*.

 A theorist may consider curriculum is a series of intended outcomes, valued learning experiences, or the way an individual learner interprets what happens in school.

(McNeil, 1976)[10]

HOME-GROWN PROGRAMS

In the end, the most powerful, meaningful, and effective curriculum may not be a "prepared" program; instead, it may be the one created by teachers and curriculum coordinators at your school site. Having teachers develop their own materials and curriculum guides on site can be more effective than a prepared package program because it matches your consensus values, content-area frameworks, and the goals and expectations for character education initiatives. We believe that prepared curriculum materials may have less of an impact than a "home-grown" curriculum. Prepared curriculum materials can be effective if they meet most of the curriculum standards on the checklist described earlier in this tour stop. Creating the character education curriculum/program at your school site may be the best way to have teachers and other school personnel take ownership. It also serves as an effective staff development experience. Character education, like critical thinking and multicultural education, should be integrated as much as possible into the existing curriculum frameworks in all of the content areas and at every grade level.

Value-a-Month Programs

Many schools develop their "home-grown" character education program using the popular "values-a-month program" (VAMP). Some schools and school districts have organized the teaching of the core values around the months of the school calendar. For instance, East View Elementary School (Oswego Community School District, No. 308, Oswego, IL) has a character education program it calls "L.I.F.E. Time: Looking Inside, Finding

Excellence," which focuses on nine monthly values, or "life skills," as it calls them. These nine values are

    September = Cooperation
    October   = Mutual respect
    November = Generosity
    December = Fairness
    January   = Perseverance
    February = Honesty
    March   = Friendship
    April   = Responsibility
    May   = Decision making

VAMP has its critics. Nevertheless, P–12 educators have found this kind of "road map" to be both helpful and practical. What can be said for VAMP, other than its popularity, is that teachers and administrators believe it provides structure, focus, and a useful plan for teaching the core values. From our discussions, it appears that this plan is popular because it helps school personnel highlight a specific value each month. It is easy to use when developing school-wide activities, classroom strategies, and parent activities. While little research supports its use, a lot of teacher, student, parent, and administrator testimonials support the plan. So, if the CEC at your school decides to use VAMP, we offer the following recommendations.

1. Beginning of the school year: The CEC should inform all stakeholders about the core values to be fostered, emphasizing the "connectedness" of all nine (one for each month) values. Students should be introduced to all the values for the year during the first two weeks of school. The council should distribute a calendar indicating suggested school-wide, classroom, and home activities for each value each month. All of the values can be addressed any time that there is a "teachable moment." All values can also be addressed during any time in a month if the value fits a "theme" on the calendar (see the following section), even if the focus is on a particular value.
2. Middle of the school year: Teachers, students, and parents review the four values highlighted during the first four months of school when school begins again after winter break. Stakeholders are reminded of the five values to be featured from January through June.

3. End of the school year: Some schools take the last two or three weeks of June, using lessons and activities, to "connect" all of the values taught and learned throughout the school year. Some schools also send home suggestions and activities so that parents can continue to emphasize the nine values during the months of July and August.

Many schools also "connect" the values with the themes of the calendar. For example, in September, we celebrate the following events:

- Children's Good Manners Month
- Back-to-School Month
- National Childhood Injury Prevention Month
- International Literacy Day
- Citizenship Day
- Labor Day
- Grandparent's Day

Kirschenbaum[11] says this about VAMP: "Teachers have many, many items to 'cover' in the course of a year's curriculum and instruction.... Many teachers and schools have attempted to solve this problem by using a 'Theme-of-the-Month' approach to organizing their values education program. Each month ... the whole school focuses on the target values.... Obviously, other important values are not ignored during the period when a class or school is focusing on the Theme-of-the-Month, but special emphasis is given to the highlighted value.... In all of these activities, there is an overlay of the values theme and, whenever possible ... (all) school personnel try to integrate the special theme into their normal activities. School continues as usual, but not really; because something very unusual is happening here. A whole school is learning values." There are as many critics as there are proponents of VAMP.

Seven Criticisms of VAMP

- Fragmented approach
- Isolated attention to individual values
- Surface level—no depth
- Educators and parents may discharge their responsibility beyond VAMP activities
- Fake, contrived approach ... (e.g., "today we will learn about honesty")

- Method is more didactic and less student-centered
- Impact may be on partial development (e.g., knowledge only)
- "Band-Aid" solution

Three Tips for Implementing VAMP

- Create communities of learners; integrate, infuse, teach, and model values all the time; simply focus a bit more specifically on the one highlighted that month.
- Highlight values/ethics as they come up in the content and provide depth in related lessons.
- Use teaching strategies, such as the seven Cs, which build character (see Tour Stop 5).

One of the major reasons why schools don't change much is that change needs Leadership . . . committed, intelligent Leadership . . .

(Goldberg, 2000)[12]

TOUR THOUGHT

What is the character education program? It is taking the values agreed upon by the school and its stakeholders and weaving those values into the life of the school. It is a reminder to all that there is more to schooling than subject matter and achievement. It reminds us that while children and youth may be exposed to "negative" values promoted by the malls, and the media, there are two places where the young will learn to be civil and caring, respectful and responsible. These places are home and school. It is here where one should find the "moral heart." "Heart is the core of human nature, the deepest motivation for moral striving. In particular, heart is the source of the fundamental impulse for relatedness. . . . In a sense, the heart . . . is like the engine which drives a person toward the realization of love."[13]

Our tour bus heads north out of San Diego along Highway 1, past Torrey Pines State Park, with the gleaming Pacific Ocean visible on our left. We eat lunch in the quaint city of Del Mar. After lunch, we head east for our meeting with the service learning coordinator at the award-winning Torrey Pines High School.[14]

We are greeted outside this beautiful school and invited in to meet teachers and students who will tell us about the service-learning programs at the school.

The tour begins with a presentation of the purposes of the program. We hear that the philosophy of the program is: "Torrey Pines will prepare its graduates to be world citizens and active community participants who give service to others, demonstrate maturity by interacting well and working cooperatively in the community, possess skills necessary to compete in a global economy and community, and be members of the global community who respect diversity."

Another presenter tells us that the program provides structured opportunities for students in three areas: (1) curriculum-related service learning; (2) club-sponsored service learning; and (3) student-initiated service learning.

The chairperson of the social students department explains how service learning is integrated into U.S. history and government classes. Throughout the year, students are provided with structured time in the regular curriculum to plan and conduct a needs assessment in the school, community, and/or city. The students continue to research and refine their projects and then perform the community-service activities related to their project. At the end of the semester, students create a reflective photo journal that documents the problem and the activities. Projects students have completed include water pollution, teen pregnancy themes, and homelessness. As a result of the "homelessness" problem, many students have volunteered to work at missions and soup kitchens.

We were told that the business department has a requirement where students complete a service-learning project by offering their computer skills to help teachers create multimedia presentations. One example, offered by the head of the science department, stated that students in an oceanography class conducted a lagoon clean-up project to study the lagoon environment and species preservation.

Student representatives of each of the following clubs made presentations. We heard about the Ambassadors Club, which sends students into the community as the high school's public relations messengers. The Earth Impact Club mobilizes all students to promote the environment and create awareness of environmental issues through such projects as recycling, beach clean-ups, tree planting, and other conservation activities. The Interact

Club engages in such projects as an annual Thanksgiving food drive and a December toy drive, and once a month members meet at a local hospice to work with the elderly.

The National Honor Society chapter members provide as many as sixty hours of service throughout the community. Roots and Shoots is a campus club that is committed to local environmental and conservation efforts. The last speaker addressing the school's club-related service learning was a student who told us about the work of the Students Against Drunk Driving (SADD).

We learned from another group of student speakers about the school's student-initiated service learning, which includes five programs. The Tutoring Center is staffed by students and offers free service to any students desiring academic assistance. The Study Buddy Program is an after-school program in which students provide friendship and tutoring to local elementary school students. The Safe Rides Program is designed to provide safe rides home to any student who is in a "dangerous" or uncomfortable situation. The Peer Assistance Listeners is a group of students who go into elementary and middle schools to do presentations that address such issues as smoking and communication skills; tutor; act as and train peer mediators; help students learn "refusal" skills; and plan dances for middle school students. The Community Volunteers Program offers students a chance to serve on a wide variety of community projects.

As the program concludes, we are told that at the end of each semester, teachers and students meet to evaluate the outcomes of each program and to get feedback from agencies that have used students' services.

J. Gauld, *Character First: The Hyde School Difference* (San Francisco, CA: ICS Press, 1993).

J. Graham, *It's Up to Us* (Langley, WA: The Giraffe Project, 1999).

D. Heath, *Schools of Hope* (San Francisco, CA: Jossey-Bass, 1994).

M. Murphy, *Character Education in America's Blue Ribbon Schools* (Lancaster, PA: Technomic, 1998).

J. Benninga, ed., *Moral, Character, and Civic Education in the Elementary School* (New York, NY: Teachers College Press, 1991).

Association for Supervision and Curriculum Development, *http://www.ascd.edu*.
Center for Civic Education, *http://www.civiced.org*.
Council for the Social Studies, *http://www.ncss.org*.
Education for Practitioners, *http://www.civnet.org*.

REFERENCES

1. R. Kanaby, "Complement to the Classroom: Willing Learners Remove Apathy from the Equation." *The High School Magazine* 4, no. 1 (1996): 8–12.
2. Editor, "Breaking Ranks: Cocurriculars Essential to Changing an American Institution." *The High School Magazine* 4, no. 1 (1996): 4.
3. J. Holloway, "Extracurricular Activities: The Path to Academic Success?" *Educational Leadership* 57, no. 4 (2000): 87–88.
4. J. Rifkin, "Rethinking the Mission of American Education." *Education Week* 15, no. 19 (1996): 32–33.
5. *Schools of Character* (New York, NY: McGraw-Hill, 1998), 18–19.
6. *Schools of Character* (New York, NY: McGraw-Hill, 1998), 20–21.
7. T. Quinn, "Weaving Values into the School Day." *Principal* 76, no. 3 (1997): 55.
8. J. D. McNeil, *Designing Curriculum: Self-Instruction Modules* (Boston, MA: Little, Brown and Company, 1976), 1–41.
9. R. C. Doll, *Curriculum Improvement: Decision Making and Process,* 8th ed. (Boston, MA: Allyn and Bacon, 1992), 272–275.
10. J. D. McNeil, *Designing Curriculum: Self-Instruction Modules* (Boston, MA: Little, Brown, and Company, 1976): 83.
11. H. Kirschenbaum, *100 Ways to Enhance Values and Morality in Schools and Youth Settings* (Needham Heights, MA: Allyn & Bacon, 1995), 96–97.
12. M. Goldberg, "An Interview with John Goodlad: Leadership for Change." *Phi Delta Kappan* 82, no. 1 (2000): 84.
13. International Educational Foundation, *Cultivating Heart & Character in the Family and School* (New York: Author, 1998), 42–43.
14. Torrey Pines High School, winner, "Blue Ribbon Schools" 1997–1998, *http://www.ed.gov/offices/OERI/BlueRibbonSchools/frames/pcah24SL.html*.

• Tour Stop 8 •

Partnerships

> *By the year 2000, every school will promote partnerships that will increase parental involvement and participation in promoting the social, emotional, and academic growth of children.*
>
> —National Education Goals Report,
> *Building a Nation of Learners* (1994)

School principals deal with two major partnerships as they go about their administrative chores. One, and the most important for character education efforts, is partnerships with parents. The second is partnerships with organizations within the community. Since the focus of this book is the school site and on you, the school's principal, our journey will take us to parents, the school's immediate community, and the school district office. We are convinced that sustained efforts to enhance partnerships that promote character education initiatives emanate from the way you organize and the leadership you and others demonstrate. Rutherford and Billig[1] write that "Leaders, both within the school and in the community[,] play a key role in fostering parent/family involvement and community involvement. Leaders set the tone for involvement, make involvement a priority, and provide the context that enables school personnel, families, community members, and businesspeople to maintain an active role...."

COMMITTEES

We recommended at Tour Stop 1 that your school form three committees (if the school site has the personnel): a character education council (CEC), a character education partnership team (CEPT), and a character education evaluation team (CEET). The CEC has the overall responsibility for the organization, implementation, and assessment of the school's partnership efforts within the character education program. The other two committees, whose chairpersons sit on the CEC, have specific tasks: (1) to work to develop partnerships and (2) to engage in program evaluation. The principal, like it or not, in our opinion, should sit on all three committees.

If the school is not large enough to form a character education partnership team (CEPT), then the CEC has to carry out these responsibilities. The point is that school personnel cannot work alone in the school's character education efforts. There must be parent and community involvement. How that gets played out is essential to the success and support of the school's character education initiatives. We have stated repeatedly that the school cannot be the "the lone ranger" in its efforts to teach personal, prosocial, and civic values to students. It is common sense that schools need parental and community help, if for no other reason than time. David Berliner[2] makes the case:

> Take the waking hours of a typical child between birth and 17 years of age (16 hours per day x 365 days per year x 17 years = 99,280 hours). Ask how many of those are school hours (6 hours per day x 180 days per year x 12 years of schooling = 12,960)? The percent of waking hours spent in neighborhoods and with family is 87 percent. The amount of time spent in schools is 13 percent.

Next, Berliner[3] asks the question, "Which socializing agency has the better chance to influence the child's attitudes, values, habits and goals?" His answer: "Clearly the family and community . . . so families and community need to be healthy. They need to provide the safety, nurturing, love and high expectations that result in school behavior that makes it easier to teach."

CEC PARTNERSHIP QUESTIONS

Experience, research, and current headlines dictate that the school has to take the lead to help parents and the many religious and public youth organizations that are in a community coordinate efforts to develop the physical, moral, and mental health of the children and youth they serve. A partnership program, when viewed through this lens, takes on new meaning. It raises the stakes. It places new responsibilities on school personnel and the leadership at the school.

The CEC, then, should address these questions as they fine-tune or develop a partnership program:

1. What are the objectives of the school's partnership program as they relate directly to the school's character education efforts (the character development of young people)?
2. Do these objectives include input from parents and community groups?
3. Do these objectives lead to collaborative and meaningful programs and activities for parents and the community?
4. To date, what objectives and activities have been accomplished? Which ones need further attention?
5. What are the CEC's plans for the next school year?
6. Are the plans designed to meet the objectives stated previously?

It may well be that the CEC cannot get beyond question 1 because it has not attended to the partnership aspect of the school's character education initiatives. Our guess is that it has some objectives and plans for parental involvement but has given little or no attention to community involvement. For purposes of making this tour stop meaningful and informative, let us separate the two. Hence, we will "tour" parent/family involvement first and then take a trip into community partnerships.

When you see real and comprehensive collaboration, you can usually find a principal and at least some teachers who were willing to lead and take risks. . . . They understand that partnership means that the school exchanges information, services, support, and benefits with its families and communities.

(Davies, 1996)[4]

PARENTS, SCHOOLS, AND CHARACTER EDUCATION

The research evidence is clear and unequivocal: parental involvement in their children's education at school increases achievement and success (Thorkildsen and Stein, 1998). We might assume that some of this success is a direct result of fostering values, such as respect, responsibility, persistence, hard work, courage, and caring at home. Some empirical evidence supports this assumption.

The best place for the school's CEC to begin its partnership journey is by attending to the National Parent Teacher Association Standards[5] for parent/family-involvement programs. We recognize that these standards do not address character education specifically, but they do provide the guidelines necessary for effective school-community partnerships. The association suggests the following six standards.

> Standard I: *Communicating*—Communication between home and school is regular, two-way, and meaningful.
> Standard II: *Parenting*—Parenting skills are promoted and supported.
> Standard III: *Student Learning*—Parents play an integral role in assisting student learning.
> Standard IV: *Volunteering*—Parents are welcome in the school, and their support and assistance are sought.
> Standard V: *School Decision Making and Advocacy*—Parents are full partners in the decisions that affect children and families.
> Standard VI: *Collaborating with Community*—Community resources are used to strengthen schools, families, and student learning.

The association offers a valuable booklet that explains each of the six standards, provides quality indicators for program success, and recommends that schools

 a. create an action team (your CEC);
 b. examine current practice (a charge for CEET);
 c. develop a plan of improvement (CEC);
 d. develop a written parent/family-involvement policy (CEC);
 e. secure support (CEC);
 f. provide professional development for school/program staff (CEC); and
 g. evaluate and revise the plan (CEC and CEET).[6]

These standards and recommendations apply to a school's partnership program. Nothing in the NPTA booklet says anything directly about character education. But its advice is applicable to efforts by you or the council to actively involve parents in the school's character education program. A true character education partnership with parents means

 a. communicating with them on a regular and sustained basis;
 b. helping them become educated about the ethical and character development of their children;
 c. working with them to reinforce at home the values being learned at school;

d. involving them in the decisions that affect the program and their children;
   e. asking them to participate in any way that meets their time and talents; and
   f. providing resources that will meet their family's needs and interests.

Elkind[7] reminds us that

> schools in postmodern times have continued the historical trend of gradually assuming parental functions.... Our schools today are providing much more in the way of child care, education for children with special needs, child support services, sex education, drug education, values education, and parent education than they did in the modern era.... If our students are doing less well academically, perhaps it is at least partly because our schools are devoting more of their resources to meeting the nonacademic needs of students.

TOURING TIPS

Studies conducted over the last 30 years have identified a relationship between parent involvement and increased student achievement, enhanced self-esteem, improved behavior, and better school attendance.

(Mapp, 1997)[8]

What can your school's CEC do to involve parents in the character education of their children? We did a tour of readings and came up with these "eleven tips for parent involvement."

1. Ensure that parents are represented on all character education councils and school committees.
2. Create a family resource center at your school.
3. Examine any language or cultural barriers that might make it difficult to communicate with parents.
4. Provide parents with a handbook of school rules and regulations.
5. Offer activities where parents, teachers, and students meet with one another.
6. Inform parents when their children demonstrate good character.
7. Provide seminars for parents on topics such as moral development, ethics, emotional growth, conflict resolution, citizenship, and violence prevention.

8. Use the talents, skills, and experiences of parents in the character education program.
9. Arrange ways that certain parents can mentor other parents.
10. Ask teachers to make special efforts to help parents foster the values being taught at school.
11. Have the CEET find out from parents what their views are about the character education program and what they need from it.

Ryan and Bohlin[9] suggest the following four tips for working with parents:

1. infusing the PTO with information about character education;
2. creating a forum where teachers, administrators, and parents can discuss issues surrounding character education;
3. drawing up parent agreements that may become the vehicle for closer communication; and
4. promoting moral conversations between parents and children by using the school's curriculum and homework assignments.

With regard to the last point, DeRoche[10] authored a booklet that includes teacher strategies and parent activities for using newspaper content to engage students in conversations about a range of personal and civic values, both at school and at home. In addition, LeGette (1999) provides twenty-one strategies for parents to use in the home to help their children develop good character.

A trip through the descriptions of award-winning schools[11] offers these additional tips:

a. Provide parents with a monthly curriculum guide that includes the theme of the month, the weekly virtue, family service suggestions, family readings, curriculum connections, and student goals.
b. Develop a Parent Resource Corps, asking parents to indicate what services they can provide.
c. Students and parents enjoy "assemblies," so offer assemblies on character education topics, including student-run assemblies.
d. To make the connection between health and character, offer parents and students programs on smoking, drug abuse, disease prevention, and mental and physical wellness.
e. Publish a community paper on character.
f. Create and publish a "caring" calendar.

g. Ask parents to support and participate in "shut off the TV night."
h. Have the PTO run special extracurricular activities and after-school programs for the students.
i. Ask teachers to weave character lessons into homework assignments that involve both parents and their children.
j. Create family nights, such as family science night, family reading night, and family arts and crafts night.
k. Use parents who have had unique "character-building" experiences to speak to the students in classes or at assemblies.
l. Create a parent volunteer program for each classroom.
m. Have a "student of the month" award for each homeroom and make the awards at a lunch with the awardees' parents invited.
n. Solicit parent help in student-led community service projects.
o. Continually check with parents about their views, their involvement, their needs, and their interest regarding the character education program.

The final "tip"—ask the parents! At some early point in the school's character education program it may be of interest to leaders and planners to get information from parents and others regarding their views about the school's character education program.

EVALUATION IDEA

Let's say that the CEET decides that it's time to find out from parents what they know about and how they perceive the school's character education program. The CEET might design a survey instrument using the following items and questions. With appropriate directions and information about how and when to return the survey form, the following items could glean useful information:

A. How would you rate your *knowledge* of this school's character education program?
1   2   3   4   5   6   7
LOW   HIGH

B. How would you rate your *involvement* in the character education programs and activities?
1   2   3   4   5   6   7
LOW   HIGH

C. How would you rate the character education *material* sent to your home?

1   2   3   4   5   6   7
CONFUSING   CLEAR

1   2   3   4   5   6   7
UNINFORMATIVE   INFORMATIVE

D. How often do you *discuss the values* with your son/daughter that the school's character education program is highlighting?

1   2   3   4   5   6   7
NEVER   OFTEN

E. To what extent *do you support* the school's efforts to teach your son/daughter personal, prosocial, and civic values?

1   2   3   4   5   6   7
LITTLE   GREAT

F. What was the last character education *activity* you attended at the school?

G. What *information* would you like about the school's character education program?

H. If you had the time to get involved in the school's character education program, *what would you like to do*?

I. What *questions* do you have about the character education program?

J. What *suggestions* can you offer for improving the character education program?

The information from an instrument like this one could be used by the CEET as discussion points if it wishes to form parent focus groups to supplement the findings from the survey. Both sets of information would help form a report to the school's CEC for action.

The future of education depends on collaborative relationships that support high expectations. But, teachers need help with navigation. Principals . . . must help teachers see that both these reform pathways can be, must be, integrated.

(Herman, 1998)[12]

THE SCHOOL AND ITS COMMUNITY

The question is this: Why should you and the CEC enter into partnerships with the community?

First: The school is just one of the organizations in the community where children and youth learn prosocial and civic values.

Second: It is no secret that many schools across this country are becoming what are called "full-service schools." In these schools there is an integration of health services, social services, and family-support services.[13]

Third: Technology has opened the school windows to the outside world.

Fourth: More and more adults are coming to the school each day for a variety of reasons. There are programs that encourage adults to tutor and mentor students, to speak to students about their experiences, and to provide guidance in life and career choices.

Fifth: The school itself has forged relationships with the community through partnership programs, sports and student performance activities, school-to-career opportunities, service-learning projects (see Tour Stop 7), and fund-raising activities.

It is probably safe to say that most schools today have some type of partnership arrangement with the community. Many schools have partnered with businesses. Others have involved community agencies and specific groups. The community is the school's resource laboratory. The question is whether the usual partnership arrangements serve the needs of the school's character education initiatives. The answer can only be determined at the school site, by the school's CEC.

THE FOUR Ds

Four steps need your attention and the CEC's planning when it comes to involving the community in character education efforts.

Step 1. Determining—It is aptly put in the musical *The Music Man:* "You gotta know the territory!" You and the CEC need to "take a tour" of the neighborhood, take "its pulse." This tour will seek out interests and concerns, determine the demographics, record the resources, identify the "power brokers," examine the issues, and answer these questions:

- What do we mean by community? Aside from parents and parent groups, do we mean businesses? . . . Youth agencies? . . . Religious groups? . . . Youth clubs? . . . And the host of community-service organizations in the community?
- How can each organization/group contribute to the mission and expectations of the program?

- How will each be invited to participate? ... By letter, by phone, by meetings?
- Will there be special requests of the media? ... Other groups?

Step 2. Discussing—Communication with the community is crucial. As principal, you need to talk with all potential contributors to the program. Equally important, you need to listen carefully to what they tell you. Because of your position as principal, you will probably be the conduit between the community and the CEC. The community will see you as the contact person. This all comes about through meetings with individuals and groups and through clear and readable written communication stripped of education jargon.

Step 3. Deciding—You and the CEC, based on the information gleaned from community conversations, must decide which policies and procedures are necessary to guide the school's partnership initiatives. The CEC needs to create policies and procedures that spell out the ground rules for community participation. The CEC also has to decide how and when groups will become involved and when and how to access their participation. Then, there is always the important decision about resources.

Step 4. Doing—The practices you decide upon will take the form of action plans. The action plans will determine how you will involve the community, what role you will expect each organization and group in the community to play, and how they can best contribute to the objectives of the school's character education program. For example, the CEC might make a list of needs and then try to match them to businesses, organizations, and groups that have expressed a willingness to become involved.

Here is a checklist of school needs that support character education initiatives:

- ☐ Help with the school's beautification efforts.
- ☐ Support student community projects.
- ☐ Provide tutors and mentors.
- ☐ Invite students to *tour* the company.
- ☐ Give time off to parents who work at the company to visit the school during the day.
- ☐ Hold special career sessions for students.
- ☐ Display students' work about the values being learned and practiced.
- ☐ Support the purchase of character education materials.
- ☐ Sponsor student recognition programs.

- ☐ Provide guest speakers for classes and assemblies.
- ☐ Support special patriotic and holiday events at the school.
- ☐ Sponsor and assist in student leadership activities.
- ☐ Serve on school council and committees.
- ☐ Participate in special efforts to reach at-risk students.
- ☐ Underwrite publications about the program.
- ☐ Support the school's student-activities program.
- ☐ Provide support for teachers to attend conferences and workshops.
- ☐ Support individual class projects that are designed to promote one or more of the core values.
- ☐ Support parent involvement activities in the program.
- ☐ Underwrite school-to-career efforts.

You and the CEC can make up your own "needs" list from this checklist and then go out into your community and find out the extent to which some or all of the needs on your list can be or will be supported by the community.

THE SCHOOL AND THE SCHOOL DISTRICT OFFICE

Little has been written about the relationship between the school and the school district office regarding character education. But do not forget them. In most cases, the community has cooperated with the school board to create a character education program, to determine the values to be fostered, and to have the schools implement and assess the program.

This typical educational "top-down" model has been, in school districts across this country, the major thrust for character education to find its way into the schools. The board authorizes the program, including the values to be taught and learned, and then tells the superintendent to do it. The superintendent, either county or district, turns it over to an individual or school team. A coordinator may be appointed. Committees are formed. Values are defined. A "value-of-the-month" plan may be adopted. Resources are allocated. Single-day or after-school workshops are offered. Curriculum guides are purchased or written. Evaluation is an afterthought. Publicity is released. Each school does something.

The district or county provides the public with the mission, goals, content and performance standards, resources, and accountability mandates. Personnel in the central office or in county offices of education have skills, talents, perspectives, and resources that should be "tapped." So, the question is: "How can they help you, the CEC and CEET, with your school's character education initiatives?" Cunningham and Cordeiro[14] offer several ways central office staff can help individual school sites. We have modified their suggestions to keep the focus on character education.

Here are ten ways that district or county personnel can help:

1. Provide background information about character education around the country.
2. Recommend plans of action.
3. Provide technical and design assistance for evaluating the program.
4. Help write teacher guides.
5. Offer ways to network with others.
6. Support your staff development needs.
7. Help with your communication efforts to other schools in the district and to parents and the community.
8. Help align the purposes of your school's character education program with the district or the school's mission and objectives.
9. Develop a curriculum center for programs used by other school districts.
10. Collect, distribute, and explain the research on character education.

TOUR THOUGHT

It seems fitting to end this tour stop on partnerships with some additional recommendations from Williamson and Johnston,[15] who have been studying parent and community concerns about middle schools. These authors make it very clear that there are certain steps that a school should follow. We found their ideas to be applicable to a school's character education program.

First, start a dialogue with the community.

Second, principals and teachers should "stop explaining" and "embrace accountability."

Third, school personnel should talk more about achievement.

Fourth, work collaboratively on a planned community-relations program.

Fifth, and one that we have talked about at Tour Stop 4, is the need to create a civil climate in schools.

The keys to parent and community partnerships are captured in the words *invitation, involvement, participation, collaboration,* and *communication.* The reason: "The efforts of schools and communities are related—children's opportunities to learn depend in part on the moral conditions around them; opportunities to become a person of strength depend, in part, on what a child learns in the course of his/her education. Educators can support community efforts by setting examples of consistently ethical, just, and kind behavior."[16]

Our tour takes us to mid-California, to the city of Visalia, where we find the offices of the Tulare County Office of Education. We are greeted by the county superintendent of schools, Jim Vidak, the visionary, driving force behind this award-winning program. Under his direction and leadership, the Tulare County Office of Education received the prestigious 2000 "Golden Ruler Award," from the International Center for Character Education at the University of San Diego. He introduces us to the man whom he has designated to coordinate this award-winning program.[17]

"My name is John Forenti. I am a 1972 graduate of Fresno State University and have been working for the Tulare County Office of Education since 1973. In 1994, I graduated from the Josephson Institute of Ethics and have been a Character Counts! coordinator for this office since 1996. Tulare County has 47 school districts, the second largest number of the 58 counties in California. Character Counts! provides these districts with one of the most comprehensive character education programs in the country.

"In 1994, Character Counts! was first used in the Tulare County Office of Education's Court/Community School program. This alternative education program serves high-risk youth, ages 13–18, who have been adjudicated by the juvenile justice system and placed on formal probation. The success of this program led Jim Vidak, superintendent of the Tulare County Office of Education, to implement the program throughout the county. Since 1996, Tulare County's Character Counts! program has sponsored national and local seminars, which have reached approximately 3,000 county citizens. Presently, over 75 percent of the school districts in the county have participated in Character Counts! activities and events. The superintendent's plan to involve members of the business community, law enforcement officials, and faith community leaders in these seminars paid tremendous dividends as Character Counts! became better known and received much support throughout the county."

As we walk over to the park to see "The Character Counts! Pillar Square Monument," Mr. Forenti describes some of the community activities that illustrate support for the program.

"The *Visalia Times Delta* newspaper has printed the names of all children in the county who have been recognized as 'Kids of Character' during national Character Counts! Week held in October of each year. Since 1996 over 2,000 youth have been recognized. In addition, stories of individual youngsters are featured during this week of celebration. In December 1999, the newspaper featured 'Kids of Character' every day that month inside its front page. The following week those youngsters' pictures appeared on our County Education Office Web site at *http://www.tcoe.org*.

"During Character Counts! Week, the California Water Service Company flies a 12 x 24 foot Character Counts! banner from its 106.50-foot tower, which stands adjacent to Mineral King Bowl, the home field to Visalia's three public high schools and College of the Sequoias, our local community college. No other banner had previously been flown from the tower. In a heartening display of support from the faith community, churches in Visalia used the 'Six Pillars of Character' as sermon topics for six consecutive Sundays. Vast numbers of Character Counts! murals are visible throughout the county. But one of the most impressive of our collaborative efforts has been with the California State *Friday Night Live* program. *Friday Night Live* is a gang, alcohol, tobacco, and drug prevention program. In 1998, the State Office adopted the Character Counts! curriculum. *Friday Night Live* reaches an estimated 750,000 school-aged youngsters throughout the State."

As we enter Mooney Groove, an eighty-acre family-oriented county park centrally located in the heart of Tulare County, to see Pillar Square Monument, we are told that the monument was erected in April 1997 at a cost of $20,000. Mr. Forenti says, "It was funded entirely by donations from the community. Labor and materials were donated. Each 'pillar' was sold for $2,000. The Deputy Sheriff's Association, the Educational Employees Credit Union, M. Green and Company, CPAs, the Tulare County Board of Supervisors, Mr. and Mrs. Michael Beans and family, and Provident Mortgage Corporation purchased a 'pillar of character' on the monument." Since its dedication, Pillar Square has been used for over thirty weddings!

Before returning to our tour bus, we thank Mr. Forenti for this informative tour demonstrating the importance of partnerships to bring character education to schools and the community. He suggests that we read the plaque on the monument before leaving the park.

> Building character is a lifelong personal and community effort. The Character Counts! Pillar Square Monument represents the dedication and commitment of the people of Tulare County to that lifelong effort. The youth of the community are one of its most loved and cherished resources. The quality of their character will be our lasting legacy.

J. Goodman, V. Sutton, and I. Harkavy, "The Effectiveness of Family Workshops in a Middle School Setting." *Phi Delta Kappan* 76, no. 9 (1995): 694–700.

E. Goldring and C. Hausman, "Parent Empowerment: The Key to Productive Partnerships." *NAESP Streamlined Seminar* 15, no. 2 (1996).

O. Graf and B. Henderson, "25 Ways to Increase Parental Participation." *The High School Magazine* 4, no. 4 (1997): 36–41.

W. Ribas, "Tips for Reaching Parents." *Educational Leadership* 56, no. 1 (1998): 83–85.

M. Sanders, "School, Family, Community Partnerships: An Action Team Approach." *The High School Magazine* 5, no. 3 (1998): 38–49.

The The Communitarian Network, *http://www.gwu.edu/~ccps*.

The National Network of Partnership-2000 Schools support the work of schools to involve families and the community, *http://www.csos.jhu.edu/p2000/*.

The National Parent Teacher Association, *http://www.pta.org*.

The National Service Learning Cooperative Clearinghouse, *http://www.nicsl.coled.umn.edu*.

REFERENCES

1. B. Rutherford and S. Billig, "Eight Lessons of Parent, Family, and Community Involvement in the Middle Grades." *Phi Delta Kappan* 77, no. 1 (1995): 66.
2. D. Berliner, "Voice Training." *UCEA Review* 38, no. 2 (1997): 14.
3. D. Berliner, "Voice Training," *UCEA Review* 38, no. 2 (1997): 14.

4. D. Davies, "The 10th School: Where School-Family-Community Partnerships Flourish." *Education Week* 10 (1996): 44.

5. National Parent Teacher Association, *National Standards for Parent/Family Involvement Programs* (Chicago, IL: National PTA, 1998), 5. Also see L. White, "National PTA Standards for Parent/Family Involvement Programs." *The High School Magazine* 5, no. 3 (1998): 8–12.

6. National Parent Teacher Association, *National Standards for Parent/Family Involvement Programs* (Chicago, IL: National PTA, 1998), 5. Also see L. White, "National PTA standards for Parent/Family Involvement Programs." *The High School Magazine* 5, no. 3 (1998): 8–12.

7. D. Elkind, "School and Family in the Postmodern World." *Phi Delta Kappan* 77, no. 1 (1995): 14.

8. K. Mapp, "Making the Connection between Families and Schools." *The Harvard Education Letter* 13, no. 5 (1997): 1.

9. K. Ryan and K. Bohlin, *Building Character in Schools* (San Francisco, CA: Jossey-Bass, 1999), 130–136.

10. E. DeRoche, *Character Matters: Strategies for Teachers, Activities for Parents* (San Francisco, CA: USETHENEWS Foundation, 2000).

11. *Schools of Character* (New York, NY: McGraw-Hill, 1998).

12. H. Thurber Herman, "Standards vs. Parent Involvement: Must We Choose Sides?" *The High School Magazine* 5, no. 3 (1998): 30.

13. J. McChesney, "Full-Service Schools." *NAESP Research Roundup* 12, no. 2 (1995 and 1996): 1–4.

14. W. Cunningham and P. Cordeiro, *Educational Administration: A Problem-Based Approach* (Boston, MA: Allyn & Bacon, 2000).

15. R. Williamson and H. Johnston, "Serious Answers to Parent/Public Middle School Concerns." *Education Digest* 64, no. 9 (1999): 6–11.

16. C. Cross, "Academic Standards or Student Safety." *Education Digest* 65, no. 2 (1999): 4.

17. Jim Vidak, Tulare County Superintendent of Schools, and John Forenti, Character Counts! Coordinator, written communication (2000).

• *Tour Stop 9* •

Evaluation

> *Schools that lack the ability to analyze their own results, that rely on outside third parties to inform them about what is working and what is not, will always be at a disadvantage. Data can drive a school to make important and evolutionary changes.*
>
> —Anderson, "Is It Working Yet?" *Education Week* 18, no. 38 (1999)

All tours are evaluated in some way. The value of a tour may be expressed anecdotally in testimonials and complaints, in the size of the tips given to the tour guide and the bus driver, and the willingness of those who have completed the tour to take another with the same company.

At this tour stop, we talk about evaluating your school's character education efforts. Our view is that evaluating character education should be done at your school, by a specific committee, involving as many stakeholders as possible, centered on question asking, using both quantitative and qualitative methods. It should be manageable, informational, and focused on the school's character education goals, expectations, and outcomes. We are not recommending "scientific" research; that is for the researchers who have different purposes than you have and whose time is devoted only to their research projects. We are recommending what Sagor[1] calls "collaborative action research." He says, "In the collaborative action research process, the focus of the research is defined by the practitioners themselves . . . (and) has five sequential steps:

1. Problem formulation,
2. Data collection,

3. Data analysis,
4. Reporting of results, and
5. Action planning."[2]

We will follow these steps in our recommendations at this tour stop. We begin with a focus on question asking. The question-asking format occurs in a primer that we recommend you and the Character Education Evaluation Team (CEET) read before engaging in evaluation work. Berkowitz (1998)[3] has written a very useful pamphlet in which he answers a series of questions about evaluating character education. Here are a few of the questions that he answers:

- Do you really know what program evaluation is?
- Why do you want to evaluate the initiative?
- Who will be the audience for the evaluation results?
- Who will do the evaluation?
- What do you want to assess?
- What types of data will you collect?
- What types of instruments can you use?

We have our own answers to these important questions, as you will note at this tour stop.

Memo to the Principal: *You are therefore advised to keep your evaluation in-house, simple, and manageable and to leave . . . (research) design to researchers whose purposes go beyond the goals and objectives for your school.*

Sincerely,
Gordon Vessels[4]

ORGANIZATION

How should you organize the stakeholders for evaluating your school's character education program? To answer this question, we propose two organizational schemes.

1. If you have a large school with many personnel, the school probably has a CEC. If this is the case, then we suggest that you also create a committee that we call the "Character Education Evaluation Team" (CEET).

2. If you lead a small school, then one committee will have to do the work required for both the program and the evaluation. In Tour Stop 1 we recommend that these tasks be assumed by the school's CEC.

The assumption we will make here is that you have enough personnel to create a separate evaluation team. Here are some recommendations:

MEMBERSHIP

You need to be on this team just as you need to be on the council. As principal, what you can bring to both committees is crucial to helping them accomplish their purposes and meet their responsibilities. CEET members should include teachers, school personnel, parents, students, representatives from the program committee (if you have one), community leaders, and special appointees such as a person from the central office, an educator from another school, or a consultant. A team of nine to twelve people is recommended, with rotating appointments over a three-year period.

PURPOSE

CEET has been formed to evaluate your school's character education efforts.

RESPONSIBILITIES

The team needs to spend time discussing their responsibilities. You need to educate team members about the value of evaluation. They need to discuss why the character education initiative needs to be evaluated and why they need to do it. The team must talk about timelines, expectations and outcomes, resources (financial and personnel), equipment, materials, and professional development opportunities to learn more about process and program evaluation.

QUESTIONS

You get good, usable, action-oriented answers by taking the time needed to pose good questions. The CEET should use the following five questions as a guide for developing answers that will direct the actions it will recommend as a result of the evaluation.

1. What is to be evaluated and why?
2. When is it to be evaluated and how will it be done?
3. Who will do the evaluation?
4. How will the data be collected and analyzed?
5. How will the findings be reported and who will receive the report?
6. What actions should occur as a result of this evaluation?

As an example of the discussions CEET members will need to have about these questions, let's examine only the question, What to evaluate and why? The answer depends on where you are in your school's character education efforts. What should be evaluated will vary from year to year. If you are in your first year, what is to be evaluated will be different than if you were in your third or fourth year.

There are three central questions that the CEET must always keep in mind:

1. *Processes:* How does the evaluation plan inform the committee members about the effectiveness of the processes used to implement, maintain, enrich, and evaluate the school's character education initiatives?
2. *Programs:* How does the evaluation plan inform the committee about the value of programmatic efforts, parent and community involvement strategies, and special school-wide and classroom activities implemented to support the school's character education efforts?
3. *Outcomes:* How does the evaluation plan inform the committee about the impact (effectiveness) of efforts to help students learn and practice the core values embedded in the school's character education program?

Of course, CEET cannot expect to evaluate all of the elements of the school's character education initiatives at the same time. The team has to decide what should be evaluated and when. Setting timelines is important. A timeline that describes a cycle of what will be evaluated over a period of three years will alert the participants to be prepared and it will enable the team to plan for and gather the resources it needs to carry out the evaluation. We recommend that no more than three elements of the character education efforts be evaluated each school year. In general, the team (with compensation) should use the summer months to analyze the data, reflect on the findings, prepare reports, design action plans for stakeholders to review, and provide feedback before changes are implemented.

What gets evaluated, gets attention.
What gets attention, gets done!

AN EVALUATION MAP: IDEAS FOR EVALUATING YOUR SCHOOL'S CHARACTER EDUCATION EFFORTS

Route One

Five key points must be highlighted here that support our suggestions and the commentary at the beginning of this tour site. Evaluating your school's character education initiatives must include:

1. the construction and use of pertinent and relevant questions;
2. the use of multiple data whenever possible when evaluating any specific factor (i.e., attendance, incidences of bullying, observations of a value in action); researchers call this "triangulation";
3. careful and thoughtful reflection about findings;
4. clear communication (writing and reporting concise answers to the questions); and
5. an opportunity for stakeholders to provide feedback to the report(s).

Route Two

Focus—that is the WHAT question! The committee has to decide WHAT is to be evaluated. Then it needs to decide WHAT the evaluation questions are. Then, WHAT evaluation methods are appropriate in order to answer the "what" questions. As we have indicated before, many factors comprise a school's character education efforts. We have listed twenty factors as an example of WHAT might be evaluated.

1. Mission and goals of the program
2. Expectations of the program
3. Core values
4. School-wide activities
5. Leadership of the program
6. Students' perceptions of the program
7. Teachers' perceptions of the program
8. Parents' perceptions of the program
9. School discipline policies
10. Resources for the program

11. Teacher strategies
12. Classroom climate
13. Community support for the program
14. School safety
15. Attendance; referrals
16. Effectiveness of the curriculum integration of the program
17. Co-curricular activities program
18. Effectiveness of staff development for the program
19. Student behavior
20. School climate

We recommend that you look at your original list of expectations and outcomes (established at Tour Stop 2) to guide the "WHAT" questions. For example, if the CEET decides to evaluate the extent to which the school's character education efforts have influenced student attendance and disciplinary reports, the committee needs to pose the "WHAT" questions: After the first year of the character education initiatives, what influence has this had, if any, on student attendance? What has happened, if anything, to the number of misbehavior referrals to the principal's office?

Route Three

Once the committee has decided what is to be evaluated, the next three "W" questions—WHO, WHEN, and WHY—must be addressed. The committee must have a discussion of WHY it wants to assess a particular element in the school's character education efforts. The WHY question provides the rationale for the evaluation and the answer(s) will eventually be useful in writing the report of findings.

The WHEN question addresses the time and resources that the committee and others can give to seeking answers to the evaluation questions. WHEN will the information be required? WHEN is the most appropriate time to collect the information needed? It will be less time-consuming, for example, to get some quantitative data such as attendance and truancy rates, disciplinary referral rates, and incidences of reported violence than it will be to solicit students' perceptions about the program. In the first case, the data is readily available. In the second, the committee has to decide how students' perceptions will be sought (survey instrument, focus groups?); will a sample of students or all students be involved? and who will collate the information and write up the findings?

Then the committee must address the WHO question. Who will be assigned the tasks of data collection, data analysis, and writing the report? The WHO question requires that the committee give careful attention to resources and timelines for its evaluation work. The committee needs to keep in mind that it can only do what it has the time and the resources to do. We urge you to remember that we are talking here about evaluation at the school site by school-site personnel. We are not talking about researchers coming to the school to do the evaluation of the character education program for you and the committee. However, the use of outside evaluators, if you have the financial resources to do it, is one strategy worth pursuing.

Route Four

HOW! That is the tough question! There are three ways to determine HOW to assess each factor in your school's character education efforts. One is to create and use your own "home-made" instruments. The other is to modify the instruments of others. The third is to use published instruments, standardized or not, for your purposes.

Our review of character education assessment methods suggests that the most popular instruments are surveys, questionnaires, scales, observations, and document and policy analysis. Again, the keys are question asking, self-evaluation, and reflection. You may recall that at Tour Stop 4, we provided a list of questions that could be used for evaluating your school's climate in four areas. We recommend that you use these questions as a reference for evaluating your school's climate.

The evaluation toolbox contains tools that are essential for the CEET. This set of "tools" contains suggestions for CEET members to keep posted as they go about their work.

CEET Evaluation Tool Box

- ☐ Examine, verify, correct/change.
- ☐ Ask good questions.
- ☐ Seek answers to the questions.
- ☐ Monitor instead of assess.
- ☐ Inquire, don't judge.
- ☐ Self-examination.
- ☐ Self-reflection.
- ☐ Self-improvement.

☐ Award no penalties or punishments.
☐ Report findings concisely and clearly.

The following set of "tools" lists a range of ways the CEET may collect data. The following list contains some of the most popular methods of collecting data for character education initiatives.

Evaluation Data Collection Tools (Check those to be used by the CEET)

☐ Testimonials
☐ Observations
☐ Anecdotes and stories
☐ Interviews
☐ Surveys
☐ Questionnaires
☐ Focus groups
☐ Journals, logs, diaries
☐ Reports: report cards, absentee rates, behavior
☐ Case studies
☐ Test results
☐ Performance data
☐ Achievement data
☐ Mapping teacher/student activities
☐ School documents and artifacts
☐ Photographs
☐ Videos
☐ Portfolios

CEET members, in using any of these methods, must prepare themselves by reading books and articles that will help them with issues such as validity and reliability of the instruments they plan to use. In addition to Berkowitz (1998)[6] and Sagor's (1992)[7] work that we referred to earlier, we recommend the following resources:

DeRoche and Williams, "Assessing Your Character Education Programs," *Educating Hearts and Minds: A Comprehensive Character Education Framework* (Thousand Oaks, CA: Corwin Press, 1998), chapter 5; and DeRoche and Williams, "Assessing Your Character Education Program," *Educating Hearts and Minds: A Comprehensive Character Education Framework*, 2d ed. (Thousand Oaks, CA: Corwin Press, 2001), chapter 6.

E. Holcomb, *Getting Excited about Data: How to Combine People, Passion, and Proof* (Thousand Oaks, CA: Corwin Press, 1999).

R. Sagor, *Guiding School Improvement with Action Research* (Alexandria, VA: Association for Supervision and Curriculum Development, 2000).

J. Sanders, *Evaluating School Programs: An Educator's Guide* (Thousand Oaks, CA: Corwin Press, 1992).

G. Vessels, *Character and Community Development: A School Planning and Teacher Training Handbook* (Westport, CT: Praeger, 1998, see appendices: "Classroom Observation Form," "School Climate Survey," "Classroom Climate Surveys," "Student Character Questionnaire—Elementary and Secondary").

G. Wiggins and J. McTighe, *Understanding by Design* (Alexandria, VA: Association for Supervision and Curriculum Development, 1998).

Before we leave this last route to talk about reporting the findings of the evaluation effort, let's take a "turn-off" on the road to share some sample instruments that you may decide to use with or without modifications.

Example One: Criteria for Effective Programs Leming,[8] in a synthesis of the research, identified nine essential criteria for an effective character education program. The CEET could use this information to evaluate the extent to which the school's program meets each or all of the criteria. The committee should do the rating first and then decide if it should ask others to rate the program. The CEET could then compare the results. An outside evaluator may also use this instrument.

Directions: Using the rating scale 1 to 5, with "1" representing *noncompliance* and "5" representing *compliance,* please circle the number that best represents your view. For any item that you rate below a "4," please give us your view of what would have to be done to rate this item a "4" or "5."

Curriculum: The program contains engaging, developmentally appropriate materials and activities.

        1   2   3   4   5

Consensus: All stakeholders in the character education process share a common perspective on the goals of character education, that is, the nature of good character.

        1   2   3   4   5

Commitment: Youth in character education programs will encounter an environment where the values and character-related behaviors are the same in all venues.

        1   2   3   4   5

Comprehensiveness: The character education effort does not end with the end of class or the school day—it pervades the child's implemented program.

        1   2   3   4   5

Competence: Teachers receive training and regular feedback regarding their role in character education to ensure a well-implemented program.

        1   2   3   4   5

Continuity: The program is not a one-shot or one-year effort; it spans a child's entire school experience.

        1   2   3   4   5

Community: Youth develop a sense of ownership of the values through democratically developed, normative consensus.

        1   2   3   4   5

Caring: The program is based on mutual respect and affection between teachers and students.

        1   2   3   4   5

Critique: The results of the program are carefully monitored; appropriate adjustments are made to ensure desired results.

        1   2   3   4   5

Example Two: Writing: An Evaluating Tool Journals, diaries, and logs were listed earlier as data collection tools for a school's character education program. Here is an example for using teacher journals to evaluate the application of respect and responsibility in the classroom. The idea comes from Richard Sagor's (1992)[9] booklet on action research. We paraphrase and embellish it here for this example.

Suppose that twenty teachers at Garner Middle School have decided to assess how the values of respect and responsibility are being implemented in their classrooms. Each teacher assumes the responsibility to spend ten to fifteen minutes after school each day for three weeks recording his or her observations about the two values. In their journals they write responses to the following prompts:

1. Describe how you tried to foster (teach) the values of respect and responsibility in class today.
2. Describe your students' behaviors and interactions regarding these two values.
3. What worked?
4. What did not work?
5. What surprised you?

6. What do *you* need to do? (relate to number 1)
7. What do your *students* need to do? (relate to number 2)

Evaluating through the use of journals, as this example shows, certainly does not consume a lot of the teachers' time. Yet, in just three weeks these teachers could generate 300 separate journal entries about teaching, learning, and practicing the values of respect and responsibility. This small investment of time and reflection, and then the recording of reflections, provides these twenty teachers with a rich source of data for analysis, discussion, and action-plan development. The action plans can then be shared with other teachers.

Example Three: Program Impact on Students In this example, the committee wants to find out how the school's character education efforts have influenced student behaviors. It decides that during the end of the second year, students, teachers, and parents will complete the following inventory, and that the findings for each group will be compared to the others to determine similarities and differences.

Directions: Please take a few minutes and answer the following questions by circling the *sign* that best represents your opinion. The *signs* are:

++ much improved   + improved a little   — no improvement
Check here if you are a: ___ student ___ teacher ___ parent

1. Have this school's character education efforts, in your opinion, resulted in students who are more:

    ++ + —   A. caring
    ++ + —   B. civil
    ++ + —   C. respectful of one another
    ++ + —   D. respectful of the property of others
    ++ + —   E. forgiving
    ++ + —   F. honest (less cheating)
    ++ + —   G. responsible for their schoolwork
    ++ + —   H. likely to follow school rules
    ++ + —   I. willing to help other students
    ++ + —   J. understanding of other's opinions
    ++ + —   K. willing to admit mistakes
    ++ + —   L. responsible for their behavior

2. Have the school's character education efforts, in your opinion, resulted in students having:

++	+	—	A. better control of their emotions
++	+	—	B. greater interest in helping others
++	+	—	C. better manners
++	+	—	D. greater sportsmanship
++	+	—	E. better understanding of choice and consequences
++	+	—	F. greater participation in school affairs
++	+	—	G. greater appreciation of the talents of other students
++	+	—	H. greater interest in schoolwork
++	+	—	I. contributed to the positive reputation of this school
++	+	—	J. received more awards than in the past
++	+	—	K. participated in more community projects/events
++	+	—	L. caused less disruption in their classes

Example Four: Using Outside Evaluators

In this example, we offer eleven questions that the CEET should consider if it plans to invite outside evaluators to the school to examine the character education program.

Before the Visit

1. What *questions* would the CEET like the evaluators to ask about the school's character education program?
2. Who are the *leaders and participants* that the CEET recommends be interviewed by the evaluators?
3. What *documents* should the evaluators examine that will define and describe this school's character education program?

After the Visit

4. What character education *projects* have the evaluators seen in the school and its classrooms that promote the mission and goals of the program?
5. What *staff practices* have the evaluators seen that foster the expectations of the school's character education program?
6. What *student activities* have the evaluators witnessed that support the character education efforts in this school?
7. What kinds of *student behaviors* have the evaluators observed?

Evaluation   161

8. What have the evaluators *heard* from those the evaluators interviewed?
9. What have the evaluators found about *parental* support and involvement in the program?
10. What have the evaluators found regarding *community* support of the character education program?
11. What have the evaluators "discovered" as a result of *interviews* (#2) that informs the processes and outcomes of this school's character education program?
12. What *recommendations* do the evaluators offer for program improvement?

These four examples suggest ways that you and the committee can construct informal, "home-made" instruments to evaluate the effectiveness of your school's character education efforts. In the first example, we shared an idea for assessing the effectiveness of your program. In the second example, we wanted to provide a way of "mapping" what teachers do to teach a particular value in their classrooms that would result in an action plan of strategies that other teachers might use. In the third example, we looked at a way to assess the perceptions of three groups regarding student behaviors as a result of the character education initiatives. And the fourth example would be useful if you enlist the help of an outside evaluator.

Route Five

Reporting

They say communication is a two-way street.... Communicating about data is more like a traffic pattern of multiple streets, some of which are two way, some one-way, and some limited to specific kinds of vehicles or special purposes like car pools.

(Holcomb, 1999)[10]

So, the committee (CEET) has done an evaluation of, let us say, three factors of the school's character education efforts. It sends the findings to the CEC. The CEC's task, along with the CEET, is to prepare a report for the stakeholders. The draft report should first go to the school committees for review and feedback before it goes "public" and findings are shared with the stakeholders. The school's CEC must solicit feedback about what the findings suggest for action.

The reporting questions are:

1. What needs to be in the report other than the findings of the evaluation?
2. How should the findings be introduced?
3. How should the findings be put in context?
4. If the report is longer than expected, will there be an executive summary?
5. Who will be the audience? Will it be the stakeholders (students, parents, and teachers)? Will it be the community (businesses, organizations, agencies, and community leaders?) . . . or both?
6. Will the media receive a copy of the report?
7. What will be the format of the report? (booklet, pamphlet, letter style)
8. Will the report tell readers what the findings suggest needs to be done at the school?

Route Six

Action Plans Evaluation should serve a purpose and the purpose is not to have a report that can be read and filed. The CEC says to the stakeholders, "Here is the report on the three factors we decided to evaluate this year; what do you recommend we do about it?" After it has feedback from the stakeholders, then the council lays out its action plans. It shares the plans, gets more feedback, and makes recommendations. The value in evaluation is that it informs action. That is, the information is used to do something—change, modify, or continue a program, activity, or strategy.

DETOUR

As we emphasized throughout this book, school sites are diverse and unique. Parents are most interested in the school in which their children are being educated and less interested in school-district matters. It is at the school site where stakeholders focus on how children are being educated and where character development takes root. We remind you, once again, that you need to think of character education in your school as an ongoing process, not simply as some definable activity or event. It is our intent to try to change the paradigm for evaluating character education from one that shifts educators' and the public's view from "testing" (achievement tests—test scores) to a process that is more open, reflective, and responsive to the unique aspects of character education efforts.

We suggest that you view the evaluation process as a way of assessing and refining the mission, expectations, programs, activities, and outcomes of your school's character education initiatives. Each refinement will require you and the program's stakeholders to make choices. Each choice leads to change. Each change requires additional evaluation. Choice and change require leadership from you and from those who are the major players in the school's character education efforts. Without leadership, the program will look like a car being driven down a one-way street, the wrong way. The driver may make it but may not know where he/she is. The driver may have to make choices on how to get back to the street that will take him/her where he/she wants to go. The driver may be flagged down by others and told to turn around. Or, the driver may crash, causing psychological and/or physical injury to himself/herself and others.

We begin our tour in Eugene, Oregon, visiting Kennedy Middle School. This school received the 1999 National Schools of Character Award from the Character Education Partnership.[11] We are met at the entrance of the school by Principal Ron Echandia and the director of school services for the district and former principal at Kennedy, Kay Mehas.

They tell us that this grade 6–8 middle school, with an enrollment of 568 students, located in one of the suburban areas of the city, experienced a turnaround in the mid-'90s when the teachers expressed concern about the climate of the school. They expressed their concerns to the School Site Council. They wanted the school to become a place where students respected one another and valued learning. Three school-improvement goals were identified—two related to the academic curriculum, the other to the school climate.

After several months of evaluation and discussion, they decided to implement the program called "Second Step" (see Tour Stop 7). Kay Mehas tell us: "It's a school-wide curriculum that teaches students skills such as how to communicate, problem-solve, and work together in a community. It actually changes their behavior. They learn the importance of responsibility and honesty . . . (and) a large section at the beginning of each unit emphasizes empathy."

Tour Stop 9

All staff members were trained to use the program and many parents and district administrators attended an all-day workshop. The faculty decided, we were told, that about forty-five minutes each Tuesday morning would be dedicated to "Second Step" lessons. One of the unique features of the plan was to have all staff members teach in a classroom. For example, a secretary team-taught with a sixth-grade teacher; a custodian did the same with an eighth-grade science teacher. The idea was to show students that the entire school community was committed to positive character development.

As the program evolved, the staff began each school year by teaching "Second Step" every day for three weeks and then having students practice the skills daily. We were given a copy of "Kennedy Schoolwide Rules" that the staff created as the program developed.

Ms. Mehas explained that "Second Step" was only one part of the school's character education program—that, as a result of the emphasis on character development, other things happened. Student leadership occurred in the creation of the Respect Committee and the Leadership Club. "Looping" (students remaining with the same teacher in seventh and eighth grades), the staff says, helps them build stronger relationships with students and parents.

Two programs were designed to "catch students doing the right thing." Every six weeks PRIDE (Personal Responsibility in Daily Efforts) recognizes qualifying students by offering them special activities, such as ice skating, movies, or swimming. Students are also recognized by earning "WOW" tickets, which are given to students who are seen doing a positive act. Tickets are put in a weekly, monthly, and yearly drawing for prizes.

We are told how the program increased parent involvement and parent volunteers. Today, Kennedy logs more parent volunteer hours than most schools in the district. In fact, one parent serves almost full-time as a volunteer coordinator.

One member of our tour group asks Ms. Mehas about program results. She tells us about changes in attitudes, school climate, and parent involvement and says that in "in 1997 only 59 percent of the students met or exceeded the state academic benchmarks while in 1998, 74 percent met or exceeded them." She also shows us information that demonstrates a dramatic decrease in antisocial behavior—in 1997 an average of 100 referrals per month; and by 1998 the average drops to 35.

As the program concludes, we hear testimonials from students, parents, and teachers. A man in the back rises to address us, saying that he is a substitute teacher and has visited every school in the district. "I can tell you that there is a definite difference when you walk into Kennedy Middle School. It is a warm and caring place."

ETS Board of Trustees, *Performance Assessment: Different Needs, Different Answers* (Princeton, NJ: Educational Testing Service, 1995).
L. Frase, F. English, and W. Posten, *The Curriculum Management Audit* (Lancaster, PA: Technomic Publishing, 1995).
J. Leming, *Character Education: Lessons from the Past, Models for the Future* (Camden, ME: Institute for Global Ethics, 1993).
K. Logan, *Getting the Schools You Want: A Step-by-Step Guide to Conducting Your Own Curriculum Management Audit* (Thousand Oaks, CA: Corwin Press, 1997).
S. Willis, ed. "Assessment That Serves Instruction: Using Assessment to Motivate Students." *Education Update* 39 (1997): 4 and 8.

Character Education Partnership (assessment database), *http://www.character.org*.

REFERENCES

1. R. Sagor, *How to Conduct Collaborative Action Research* (Alexandria, VA: Association for Supervision and Curriculum Development, 1992), 9.

2. R. Sagor, *How to Conduct Collaborative Action Research* (Alexandria, VA: Association for Supervision and Curriculum Development, 1992), 10.

3. M. Berkowitz, *A Primer for Evaluating a Character Education Initiative* (Washington, DC: The Character Education Partnership, 1998).

4. G. Vessels, *Character Education and Community Development* (Westport, CT: Praeger, 1998), 165.

5. J. Anderson, "Is It Working Yet? *Education Week* 18, no. 38 (1999): 30.

6. M. Berkowitz, *A Primer for Evaluating a Character Education Initiative* (Washington, DC: The Character Education Partnership, 1998).

7. R. Sagor, *How to Conduct Collaborative Action Research* (Alexandria, VA: Association for Supervision and Curriculum Development, 1992).

8. J. Leming, *Character Education: Lessons from the Past, Models for the Future* (Camden, ME: Institute for Global Ethics, 1993), 29–30.

9. R. Sagor, *How to Conduct Collaborative Action Research* (Alexandria, VA: Association for Supervision and Curriculum Development, 1992).

10. E. Holcomb, *Getting Excited about Data: How to Combine People, Passion, and Proof* (Thousand Oaks, CA: Corwin Press, 1999).

11. The Character Education Partnership, National Schools of Character Awards (1999), *http://www.character.org/schools/index.cgi?detail:month.*

Character-Education Organizations

We understand that Web site links, along with phone numbers and addresses, change over time. To ensure that the links are current, we direct you to the ICCE Web site at the University of San Diego for frequent updates: *http://teachvalues.org*. You can bookmark the ICCE Web site to use it to click through to the character-education organizations listed here.

CHARACTER EDUCATION ASSOCIATIONS, INSTITUTES, CENTERS, AND NETWORKS

Center for the Advancement of Ethics and Character, School of Education, Boston University, 605 Commonwealth Avenue, Boston, MA 02215; Tel: (617) 353-3262; Fax: (617) 353-4351; *http://www.bu.edu/education/caec*.

Center for Civic Education, 5146 Douglas Fir Road, Calabasas, CA 91302-1467; Tel: (818) 591-9321; Fax: (818) 591-9330; *http://www.civiced.org*.

The Center for Collaborative Education: An Affiliate of the Coalition of Essential Schools, 1573 Madison Ave., Rm. 201, New York, NY 10029-3899; Tel: (212) 348-7821; Fax: (212) 348-7850; *http://www.cce.org*.

Center for Learning, 21590 Center Ridge Road, Rocky Road, OH 44116; Tel: (216) 331-1404; Fax: (216) 331-5414; *http://www.centerforlearning.org*.

Center for the 4th and 5th Rs, P.O. Box 2000, SUNY, Cortland, Education Department, Cortland, NY 13045; Tel: (607) 753-2455; Fax: (607) 753-5980; *http://www.cortland.edu/www/c4n5rs*.

Character Development Foundation, P.O. Box 4782, Manchester, NH 03108-4782; Tel/Fax: (603) 472-3063; *http://www.charactered.org*.

Character Development Group, P.O. Box 9211, Chapel Hill, NC 27515-921; Tel: (919) 967-2110; Fax: (919) 967-2139; *http://www.charactereducation.com*.

Character Education Institute, 8918 Tesoro Drive, Suite 575, San Antonio, TX 78217-6253; Tel: (800) 284-0499; Fax: (210) 829-1729; http://www.character education.org.

Character Education Institute at California University, 250 University Avenue, Box 75, California, PA 15419-1394; Tel: (724) 938-4500; Fax: (724) 938-4156; http://www.cup.edu/character.ed.

Character Education Partnership, 1025 Connecticut Ave. Suite 1011, Washington, DC 20036; Tel: (800) 988-8081; Fax: (202) 296-7779; http://www.character.org.

Character Plus [formerly PREP], Cooperating School Districts, 8225 Florissant Rd., St. Louis, MO 63121; Tel: (314) 692-9728 or (800) 478-5684x 4522; Fax: (314) 516-4599; http://info.csd.org/staffdev/chared/characterplus.html.

Civitas Associates, 232 No. Kingshighway, #2101 St. Louis, MO 63108-4002; Tel: (341) 367-6480; Fax: (314) 367-7742; http://www.civitas-stL.com/.

The Communitarian Network, 2130 H Street, N.W., Suite 703, Washington, DC 20052; Tel: (202) 994-7997; http://gwu.edu/~ccps.

Community of Caring, Joseph P. Kennedy Jr. Foundation, 1325 G Street, N.W., Washington, DC 20005; Tel: (202) 393-1251; Fax: (202) 824-0351; http://www.communityofcaring.org.

The Consortium for Social Responsibility and Character in Education, University of Central Florida, College of Education, Suite ED-318, P.O. Box 161992, Orlando, FL 32816-1992; Tel: (407) 823-3819; Fax: (407) 823-5135; http://ucfed.ucf.edu/csfce.

The Council for Global Education, P.O. Box 57218, Washington, DC 20036-9998; Tel: (202) 496-9780; Fax: (202) 496-9781; http://www.globaleducation.org.

Developmental Studies Center, 2000 Embarcadero, Suite 305, Oakland, CA 94606-5300; Tel: (510) 533-0213; Fax: (510) 464-3670; http://www.devstu.org.

Educators for Social Responsibility, 23 Garden Street, Cambridge, MA 02138; Tel: (800) 370-2515; Fax: (617) 864-5164; http://www.esrnational.org.

Ethics Resource Center, 1747 Pennsylvania Avenue, N.W., Suite 400, Washington, DC 20005; Tel: (202) 737-2258, Fax: (202) 737-2227; http://www.ethics.org.

The Institute for Global Ethics, 11/13 Main Street, P.O. Box 563, Camden, ME 04843; Tel: (207) 236-6658; Fax: (207) 236-4014; http://www.globalethics.org.

International Center for Character Education, University of San Diego, 5998 Alcala Park, San Diego, CA 92110-2492; Tel: (619) 260-5980; Fax: (619) 260-7480; http://teachvalues.org.

International Educational Foundation, 4 West 43rd Street, New York, NY 10036; Tel: (212) 944-7466; Fax: (212) 944-6683; www.iefcharactered.org.

Josephson Institute of Ethics, 4640 Admiralty Way, Suite 1001, Marina del Rey, CA 90292-6610; Tel: (310) 306-1868, Fax: (310) 827-1864; http://www.josephsoninstitute.org.

The Kenan Ethics Program, Duke University, Box 90432, 102 West Duke Building, Durham, NC 27708; Tel: (919) 660-3033; Fax: (919) 660-3049; http://kenan.ethics.duke.edu.

Moral Development Education, AERA-SIG Moral Development and Education; http://www.unikonstanz.de/SIG-MDE/-top.

Quest International, 1984 Coffman Road, P.O. Box 4850, Newark, OH 43058-4850; Tel: (614) 522-9165; http://www.quest.edu.

School for Ethical Education, 440 Wheelers Farm Road, Milford, CT 06460; Tel: (203) 783-4439; Fax: (203) 783-4461; http://www.ethicsed.org.

Other Associations Supportive of Character Education

American Association of Colleges of Teacher Education, 1307 New York Ave., N.W., Suite 300, Washington, DC 20005-4701; Tel: (202) 293-2450; Fax: (202) 457-8095; http://www.aacte.org.

American Association of School Administrators, 1801 North Moore Street, Arlington, VA 22209-9988; Tel: (703) 528-0700, Fax: (703) 841-1543; http://www.aasa.org.

American Federation of Teachers, 555 New Jersey Avenue, N.W., Washington, DC 20001; Tel: (202) 879-4400; http://www.aft.org.

American Youth Foundation, 2331 Hampton Avenue, St. Louis, MO 63139; Tel: (314) 646-6000, Fax: (314) 772-7542; http://www.ayf.com.

Association for Moral Education, c/o Darcia Narvaez, Secretary, College of Education and Human Development, University of Minnesota, 206 Burton Hall—178 Pillsbury Drive, S.E., Minneapolis, MN 55455; http://www4.wittenberg.edu/ame/index.html.

Association for Supervision and Curriculum Development, 1703 North Beauregard Street, Alexandria, VA 22311-1714; Tel: (800) 933-ASCD; Fax: (703) 575-5400; http://www.ascd.org.

Association of Teacher Educators, 1900 Association Drive, Suite ATE, Reston, VA 20191-1502; Tel: (703) 620-3110; Fax: (703) 620-9530; http://www.siu.edu/departments/coe/ate.

The Boyer Center, Tel: (717) 796-5077; Fax: (717) 796-5081; http://www.boyercenter.org.

Basic Schools Network, University of Missouri-Columbia, 202 Hill Hall, Columbia, MO 65211; Tel: (816) 235-2454; Fax: (816) 235-6511; http://basicschool.coe.missouri.edu.

Center for Youth Citizenship (CYC), 9738 Lincoln Village Drive, Sacramento, CA 95827; Tel: (916) 228-2322; Fax: (916) 228-2493; http://www.clre.org.

Close-Up Foundation, 44 Canal Center Plaza, Alexandria, VA 22314; Tel: (703) 706-3330; Fax: (703) 706-0001.

The Committee for Children, 2203 Airport Way S., Suite 500, Seattle, WA 98134-2027; Tel: (800) 634-4449 or (206) 343-1223; Fax: (206) 343-1445; http://www.cfchildren.org/reachus.htm.

The Jean Piaget Society, Department of Human Development, Graduate School of Education, Larsen Hall, Harvard University, Cambridge, MA 02138; http://www.piaget.org.

Learn and Serve America, Corporation for National Service, 1201 New York Avenue, N.W., Washington, DC 20525; Tel: (202) 606-5000; http://www.cns.gov/learn/index.html.

170   Character–Education Organizations

Learning for Life, Boy Scouts of America, 1325 West Walnut Hill Lane, P.O. Box 152079, Irving, TX 75015-2079; Tel: (972) 580-2000; http://www.learning-for-life.org.

National Association of Partners in Education, 901 No. Pitt Street, Suite 320, Alexandria, VA 22314; Tel: (703) 836-4880; Fax: (703) 836-6941; http://www.napehq.org.

National Association of Secondary School Principals, 1904 Association Drive, Reston, VA 22191-1537; Tel: (800) 860-0200; Fax: (703) 476-5432; http://www.nassp.org.

National Council for the Social Studies, 3501 Newark Street, N.W., Washington, DC 20016; Tel: (202) 966-7840; Fax: (202) 966-2061; http://www.ncss.org.

National Education Association, Suite 800, 1201 Sixteenth Street, N.W., Washington, DC 20036; Tel: (202) 833-4000; http://www.nea.org.

National School Boards Association, 1680 Duke Street, Alexandria, VA 22314; Tel: (703) 838-6722; (703) 683-7590; http://www.nsba.org.

National Youth Leadership Council, 1910 West County Road B, Roseville, MN 55113; Tel: (651) 631-3672; Fax: (651) 631-2955; http://www.nylc.org.

Northeast Foundation for Children, 71 Montague City Road, Greenfield, MA 01301; Tel: (800) 360-6332; Fax: (413) 772-2097.

Phi Delta Kappa International, 408 N. Union St., P.O. Box 789, Bloomington, IN 47402-0789; Tel: (800) 766-1156; Fax: (812) 339-0018; http://www.pdkintl.org.

The Sangreal Group, 1309 Linda Vista St., Suite 80, Orange, CA 92869; Tel: (800) 598-7073; http://www.sangreal-group.com.

Southern Poverty Law Center, 400 Washington Ave., Montgomery, AL 36104; Tel: (334) 264-0286; Fax: (334) 264-3121; http://www.splcenter.org.

Youth Service America, 1101 15th Street, Suite 200, Washington, DC 20005; Tel: (202) 296-2992 x43; Fax: (202) 296-4030; http://www.ysa.org.

Character Education Programs and Materials

Child Development Project—Developmental Studies Center, 2000 Embarcadero, Suite 305, Oakland, CA 94606-5300; Tel: (510) 533-0213; Fax: (510) 464-3670; http://www.devstu.org.

Do Something, 423 West 55th Street, 8th Floor, New York, NY 10019; Tel: (212) 523-1175; Fax: (212) 582-1307; http://www.dosomething.org.

The Giraffe Project, P.O. Box 759, 197 Second Street, Langley, WA 98260; Tel: (360) 221-7989; Fax: (360) 221-7817; http://www.giraffe.org.

The Heartwood Ethics Institute, 425 North Craig Street, Suite 302, Pittsburgh, PA 15213; Tel: (800) HEART-10; Fax: (412) 688-8570; http://www.heartwoodethics.org.

Elkind & Sweet Communications/Livewire Video, 3450 Sacramento Street, San Francisco, CA 94118; Tel: (415) 759-3904, Fax: (415) 665-8006; *http://www.goodcharacter.com.*

Jalmar Press, 24426 S. Main Street, Unit 702, Carson, CA 90745; Tel: (310) 816-3085; Order number: (800) 662-9662; *http://www.jalmarpress.com.*

National Professional Resources, 25 South Regent St., Port Chester, NY 10573; Tel: (800) 453-7461; Fax: (914) 937-9327; *http://www.nprinc.com.*

Positive Action Company, 321 Eastland Drive, Twin Falls, ID 83301; Tel: (800) 345-2974; Fax: (208) 733-1590.

Project Wisdom; Tel: (800) 884-4974; Fax: (793) 664-6944; *http://www.projectwisdom.com*

School Development Program, Yale Child Study Center, 55 College Street, New Haven, CT 06510; Tel: (203) 737-1020; Fax: (203) 737-1023; *http://www.pandora.med.yale.edu/comer/welcome.html.*

Wise Skills, PO Box 491, Santa Cruz, CA 95061; Tel: (888) WISESKILLS (1-888-947-3754); Fax: (831) 426-8930; *http://www.wiseskills.com.*

Bibliography

Anderson, J., "Is It Working Yet?" *Education Week* 18, no. 38 (1999): 30.
Berliner, D., "Voice Training." *UCEA Review* 38, no. 2 (1997): 10–11, 14–15.
Berkowitz, M., *A Primer for Evaluating a Character Education Initiative.* Washington, DC: The Character Education Partnership, 1998.
Birman, B. F., L. Desimone, A. C. Porter, and M. S. Baret, "Designing Professional Development That Works." *Educational Leadership* 8, no. 57: 29.
Bohlin, K., in S. S. Cohen, "The Moral Future of Our Children." *Parents* 75, no. 2 (2000): 86–92.
Bosworth, K., "Caring for Others and Being Cared for." *Phi Delta Kappan* 26, no. 9 (1995): 686–693.
Boyer, E. L., *The Basic School: A Community for Learning.* Princeton, NJ: The Carnegie Foundation for the Advancement of Teaching, 1995.
Bridges, W., *Managing Transitions.* Boston: Addison-Wesley, 1991.
Brooks, J. G., and M. G. Brooks, *In Search of Understanding: The Case for Constructivist Classrooms.* Alexandria, VA: Association for the Supervision and Curriculum Development, 1993.
Bruner, J., *Toward a Theory of Instruction.* Cambridge, MA: Harvard University Press, 1966.
Center for Civic Education, *The Role of Civic Education: A Report of the Task Force on Civic Education.* Calabasas, CA: author, 1995
Character Education Manifesto. Center for the Advancement of Ethics and Character, *http://education.bu.edu/charactered*, 1998.
Chula Vista Elementary School District, *Principal Standards: Working Document.* Author, 2000. Consortium on Renewing Education, "Forum." *Education Week* 18, no. 12 (December 1998): 24.
Cross, C., "Academic Standards or Student Safety." *Education Digest* 65, no. 2 (1999): 4–5.

Cunningham, W., and P. Cordeiro, *Educational Administration: A Problem-Based Approach.* Boston: Allyn & Bacon, 2000.

Dalton, J., and M. Watson, *Among Friends: Classrooms Where Caring and Learning Prevail.* Oakland, CA: Developmental Studies Center, 1997.

Darling-Hammond, L., and M. McLaughlin, "Policies That Support Professional Development in an Era of Reform." In M. McLaughlin and I. Oberman, eds., *Teacher Learning: New Policy, New Practices.* New York: Teachers College Press, 1996.

Davies, D., "The 10th School: Where School-Family-Community Partnerships Flourish," *Education Week* 10 (1996): 44.

Deal, T., and Peterson K., *Five Key Roles That Principals Play in Shaping a School's Culture* (1998).

DeRoche, E., *An Administrator's Guide for Evaluating Programs and Personnel.* Boston: Allyn & Bacon, 1981.

——— *Character Matters: Strategies for Teachers, Activities for Parents.* San Francisco: USETHENEWS Foundation, 2000.

DeRoche, E. F., and M. M. Williams, *Educating Hearts and Minds: A Comprehensive Character Education Framework.* Thousand Oaks, CA: Corwin Press, 1998.

——— *Educating Hearts and Minds: A Comprehensive Character Education Framework,* 2d ed. Thousand Oaks, CA: Corwin Press, 2001.

DeVries, R., and B. Zan, *Moral Classrooms, Moral Children.* New York: Teachers College Press, 1994.

Drucker, P., *Post-Capitalist Society.* New York: HarperCollins, 1993.

Editor, "Breaking Ranks: Cocurriculars Essential to Changing an American Institution." *The High School Magazine* 4, no. 1 (1996): 4.

Elkind, D., "School and Family in the Postmodern World." *Phi Delta Kappan* 77, no. 1 (1995): 14.

Elkind, D., and F. Sweet, "The Socratic Method to Character Education." *Educational Leadership* (May 1997): 56–59.

Etzioni, A. "The Truths We Must Face to Curb School Violence." *Education Week* 18, no. 39 (1999): 57.

Fitch, C., "School Organization and Class Scheduling: Conventional and Reformed," ed. J. Kaiser. In *The 21st Century Principal.* Mequon, WI: Stylex, 1995, 111, 115.

French, D., "The State's Role in Shaping a Progressive Vision of Public Education." *Phi Delta Kappan* 80, no. 3 (1998), 193.

Glasser, W., *The Quality School: Managing Students without Coercion.* New York: HarperCollins, 1985.

Good, T. L., and J. E. Brophy, *Looking in Classrooms,* 8th ed. New York: Longman, 2000.

Gordon, T., *T.E.T.—Teacher Effectiveness Training.* New York: Peter H. Wyden, 1974.

Hansen, J. M., and J. Childs, "Creating a School Where People Like to Be." *Educational Leadership* 56, no. 1 (1998): 14–17.

Hawley, W., and L. Valli, "The Essentials of Effective Professional Development: A New Consensus." Paper presented at the AERA Invitational Conference on Teacher Development and School Reform, Washington, DC, April 1996.

Heifetz, R., *Leadership without Easy Answers.* Cambridge, MA: Harvard University Press, 1994.

Holcomb, E., *Getting Excited about Data: How to Combine People, Passion, and Proof.* Thousand Oaks, CA: Corwin Press, 1999.

Holloway, J., "Extracurricular Activities: The Path to Academic Success?" *Educational Leadership* 57, no. 4 (2000): 87–88.

Huffman, H., *Developing a Character Education Program: One School District's Experience.* Alexandria, VA: Association for Supervision and Curriculum Development, 1994.

International Educational Foundation, *Cultivating Heart & Character in the Family and School.* New York: Author, 1998.

Jackson, P., R. Boostrom, and D. Hansen, *The Moral Life of Schools.* San Francisco: Jossey-Bass, 1993.

Janofsky, M., "A Bright Light in a City Shadowed by Trouble." *New York Times,* 28 September 1997, 10.

Johnson, D. W., R. T. Johnson, E. J. Holubec, and P. Roy, *Circles of Learning: Cooperation in the Classroom.* Alexandria, VA: Association for Supervision and Curriculum Development, 1984.

Kanaby, R., "Complement to the Classroom: Willing Learners Remove Apathy from the Equation." *The High School Magazine* 4, no. 1 (1996): 8–12.

Keller, B., "Principal Matters." *Education Week 18,* no. 11 (November, 1998): Leadership Characteristics.

Kilpatrick, W., "cover quote." In E. Wynne and K. Ryan, *Reclaiming Our Schools: A Handbook on Teaching Character, Academics, and Discipline.* New York: Macmillan Publishing Co., 1993.

Kirschenbaum, H., *100 Ways to Enhance Values and Morality in Schools and Youth Settings.* Needham Heights, MA: Allyn & Bacon, 1995.

Kohn, A., *The Schools Our Children Deserve.* Boston: Houghton Mifflin, 1999.

LeGette, H., *Parents, Kids, and Character.* Chapel Hill, NC: Character Development Publishing, 1999.

Lehmann, H., *Driver's Ed for Today's Managers.* Auburn, WA: Organizational Performance & Planning Institute, 1998.

Leming, J., *Character Education: Lessons from the Past, Models for the Future.* Camden, ME: The Institute for Global Ethics, 1993.

———. "Current Evidence Regarding Program Effectiveness in Character Education: A Brief Review." In *Character Education: The Foundation for Teacher Education,* ed. M. Williams and E. Schaps. Washington, DC: Character Education Partnership, 1999, 50–54.

———. "Applied Ethics or Character Education?: Contrasting Approaches to the Development of Moral Teachers." Paper presented at the annual meeting of the American Association of Colleges of Teacher Education, Chicago, February 2000.

Lewis, A. C., "A New Consensus Emerges on the Characteristics of Good Professional Development." In *The Best of the Harvard Education Letter: Meeting the Challenges of Reform*. Cambridge, MA: Harvard Education Publishing Group (n.d.), 6.

Lickona, T., *Educating for Character: How Our Schools Can Teach Respect and Responsibility.* New York: Bantam Books, 1991.

Lunenburg, F., and A. Ornstein, *Educational Administration*. Belmont, CA: Wadsworth, 2000.

Mapp, K., "Making the Connection between Families and Schools." *The Harvard Education Letter* 13, no. 5 (1997): 1.

McChesney, J., "Full-Service Schools." *NAESP Research Roundup* 12, no. 2 (1995 and 1996): 1–4.

McNeil, J. D., *Designing Curriculum: Self Instruction Modules*. Boston, MA: Little, Brown and Company, 1976.

Merrill, M. D., "Constructivism and Instructional Design." *Educational Technology* (1991): 45–53.

Moffett, C., "Resistance to Change: Taking a Closer Look." *Professional Development Newsletter.* Alexandria, VA: Association for Supervision and Curriculum Development (1995), 8.

National Education Goals Report, *Building a Nation of Learners,* Goal 8 (1994).

National Parent Teacher Association, *National Standards for Parent/Family Involvement Programs.* Chicago, IL: National PTA, 1998, 5.

O'Donnell, M., "Boston's Lewenberg Middle School Delivers Success." *Phi Delta Kappan* 78, no. 7 (1997): 508–512.

Quinn, T., "Weaving Values into the School Day." *Principal* 76, no. 3 (1997): 54–55.

Rifkin, J., "Rethinking the Mission of American Education." *Education Week* 15, no. 19 (1996): 32–33.

Robinson, S., in A. C. Lewis, "A New Consensus Emerges on the Characteristics of Good Professional Development." In *The Best of the Harvard Education Letter: Meeting the Challenges of Reform*. Cambridge, MA: Harvard Education Publishing Group, (n.d.).

Rutherford, B., and S. Billig, "Eight Lessons of Parent, Family, and Community Involvement in the Middle Grades." *Phi Delta Kappan* 77, no. 1 (1995): 64–68.

Ryan, K., and Bohlin, K., *Building Character in Schools*. San Francisco, CA: Jossey-Bass, 1999.

Sagor, R., *How to Conduct Collaborative Action Research*. Alexandria, VA: Association for Supervision and Curriculum Development, 1992.

Salomone, R., "Education for Democratic Citizenship." *Education Week* 19, no. 2: 48, 52.

Schaps, E., "Community in School: A Key to Violence, Character Formation, and More." *Character Education* 8, no. 2 (2000): 1.

Schaps, E., and C. Lewis, "Breeding Citizenship through Community in School." *Education Digest* 64, no. 1 (1998): 24.

Schaps, E., C. Lewis, and M. Watson, "Building Community in School." *Principal* 76, no. 2 (1996): 22–24.

Schaps, E., T. Lickona, and C. Lewis, *The 11 Principles*. Washington, DC: The Character Education Partnership.

Schools of Character. New York: McGraw-Hill, 1998.

Sockett, H., *The Moral Base for Teacher Professionalism*. New York: Teachers College Press, 1993.

Sterling, M., "Building a Community Week by Week." *Educational Leadership* 56, no. 1 (1998): 65–68.

Talbot, M., and N. Tate, "Shared Values in a Pluralist Society?" In *Teaching Right and Wrong: Moral Education in the Balance,* ed. R. Smith and P. Standish. Great Britain: Cromwell Press Ltd. (1997), 1–14.

Tell, C., "Generation What? Connecting with Today's Youth," *Educational Leadership* 57, no. 4 (2000): 8–12.

Thorkildsen, R., and M. Stein, "Is Parent Involvement Related to Student Achievement?" *PDK Research Bulletin* 22: (December 1998) 17–20.

Vessels, G., *Character Education and Community Development*. Westport, CT. Praeger, 1998.

White, L., "National PTA Standards for Parent/Family Involvement Programs." *The High School Magazine* 5, no. 3: 8–12.

Wiggins, G. "The Futility of Trying to Teach Everything of Importance." *Educational Leadership* 47, no. 3: 44–48.

Williams, M. M., "Actions Speak Louder Than Words: What Students Think about Character Education." *Educational Leadership* 51, no. 3 (November 1993): 22–23.

Williams, M. M., and E. Schaps, eds., "Character Education." *Action in Teacher Education*. Alexandria, VA: Association of Teacher Education, 1999a.

——— *Character Education: The Foundation for Teacher Education*. The Report of the ATE National Commission on Character Education. Washington, DC: Character Education Partnership, 1999b.

Williamson, R., and H. Johnston, "Serious Answers to Parent/Public Middle School Concerns." *Education Digest* 64, no. 9 (1999): 4–11.

Wynne, E. A., "Looking at Good Schools." In *Kaleidoscope: Readings in Education,* ed. K. Ryan and J. Cooper. Boston: Houghton Mifflin, 1998: 201–209.

Zigler, Z. "Cover quote." In B. D. Brooks and Frank G. Goble, *The Case for Character Education: The Role of the School in Teaching Values and Virtue*. Northridge, CA: Studio 4 productions, 1997.

About the Authors

Edward F. DeRoche joined the University of San Diego's School of Education as dean in 1979 and returned to the faculty as professor and co-director of the International Center for Character Education in 1998. He received a B.A. from the University of Maine and an M.Ed. from Eastern Connecticut State University. From the University of Connecticut, he earned an M.A. and a Ph.D.

Ed was an elementary and junior high school teacher and principal, a member of a public school board of education, and he has served on several private school boards. He has been president of the California State Association of Teacher Educators and a member of the California Commission on Teacher Credentialing. He served as a member of the National Commission on Character Education for the Association of Teacher Educators. He is a consultant, speaker, evaluator, author, teacher trainer, and recipient of several awards. Besides teaching courses and conducting workshops on character education, Ed has published more than fifty articles in education journals and many articles in daily newspapers.

His list of books include: *Creative Problem-Solving Techniques for Teachers and Students; Real World Reading Activities for Teachers and Students* (co-authored); *Project Update: The Newspaper in the Elementary and Junior High School Classroom; The Newspaper: A Reference Book for Teachers and Librarians; 400 Group Games and Activities for Teaching Math* (co-authored); *How School Administrators Solve Problems; A Complete Guide To Administering School Services* (co-authored); *Public Speaking Handbook for School Administrators; An Administrator's Guide for Evaluating School Programs and Personnel* (two editions); and *Character Matters: Using Newspapers to Teach Values.*

About the Authors

Mary M. Williams received a B.S. degree in Elementary Education from the State University of New York (SUNY), Plattsburgh, an M.S. degree in Reading K-12 from SUNY, Albany, and an Ed.D in Educational Leadership: Curriculum, Instruction, and Supervision from Boston University.

Mary was an Associate Professor at Pace University in New York. She is currently a professor of Education at the University of San Diego, and co-founder, co-director of USD's International Center for Character Education. She was co-chair of the National Commission on Character Education (1997-2000).

Mary has been a teacher (K-12), reading specialist, curriculum coordinator, staff developer, teacher educator, and a program evaluator. She conducts regional and national workshops, and makes presentations in character development, ethical issues in education, case-based pedagogy, literacy and diversity issues, technology, and authentic assessment.

Mary has published numerous articles including: "Actions Speak Louder Than Words: How Students View Character Education" in *Educational Leadership* (11/93); "Leadership in Character Education: A Framework for Teaching Values and Ethics" in *Education International* (6/00); and "Models of Character Education: Perspectives and Developmental Issues" in the *Journal of Humanistic Counseling, Education and Development* (9/00). She is co-author of *Educating Hearts and Minds: A Comprehensive Character Education Framework (2nd Edition),* and co-editor of *Character Education: The Foundation of Teacher Education,* the report of the National Commission on Character Education.